MOONSHOT APPLIED

SUSTAINING EXCEPTIONAL INNOVATION AT SCALE

BRETT SAVILL AND PETER ROSSDEUTSCHER

Copyright © 2023 by Peter Rossdeutscher and Brett Savill

First published in Australia by Atomic Sky 2023
The moral right of the authors has been asserted.

All rights reserved. No part of this publication may be reproduced in any form, stored in a retrieval system, or transmitted in any form or by any means, electronic, mechanical, photocopying, recording or otherwise without written permission from the publisher or author.

Moonshot Applied
ISBN: 978-0-6459631-0-6

Cover and Editorial Design: Naomi Rossdeutscher,
House of Paradox

Editor: Sarah Endacott

Special thanks to Erica Smyth for her feedback

Although this publication is designed to provide accurate information in regard to the subject matter covered, the publisher and the author assume no responsibility for errors, inaccuracies, omissions, or any other inconsistencies herein. This publication is meant as a source of valuable information for the reader, however it is not meant as a replacement for direct expert assistance.

Foreword

Adrian Beer, Managing Director, Australian Innovation Exchange (AIX) said, "Companies that are bold and invest in innovation typically outperform their peers in terms of revenue growth, profitability, and stakeholder engagement. But what is innovation in today's rapidly changing business environment? Net zero, sustainability, autonomy, big data, and AI are fundamentally impacting all sectors, making innovation strategies critical for success.

True innovation leaders aren't defined by one brilliant insight or being first to market, rather they foster conscious, consistent experimentation and collaboration within their organizations and with external stakeholders. Moonshot Applied draws upon decades of shared experience of Peter and Brett, working with industry leaders and serial innovators to uncover the key drivers for investing and scaling innovation. They delve into the ingredients of success, understanding how to effectively leverage emerging and evolving technologies, spot, and scale innovation, and what it takes to partner with start-ups and ecosystem stakeholders to realise true innovation. Real-world examples showcase companies with innovative strategies that drive growth, keeping them ahead of the competition.

Whether you're a board member initiating conversations, an executive or leader looking to innovate better, or simply interested in the topic, this book offers practical guidance, insights, and tools to harness the power of innovation for success. Peter and Brett also share their own first-hand experiences to deliver high-impact corporate innovation and growth. Happy innovating!"

Adrian has thirty years' experience in industrial technology across a range of capital-intensive industries. Prior to leading the Growth Centre, he held global executive strategy roles within two of the world's largest industrial technology organisations.

Preface

Moonshot Applied provides profound insights into corporate innovation and extends valuable guidance to proven tools and processes that support implementation. Peter Rossdeutscher and Brett Savill are seasoned executives, entrepreneurs, and trusted advisors. They have authored this comprehensive guide drawing from valuable lessons, interviews, and corporate case studies.

This book delves into the process of achieving excellence through innovation. It pragmatically sheds light on how thriving companies leverage both vision and execution to consistently identify, nurture, and bring about meaningful strategic outcomes.

The most successful innovators set bold aspirations and ambitious objectives, underpinned by a strategic thesis that factors the impact of exponential technologies, shifting customer behaviours, and emerging business models. These organisations allocate substantial resources to innovation, underpinned by a readiness to embrace tools like open innovation and purposeful collaborations.

Moonshot Applied shows how the world's top-performing organisations combine audacious ambition with impeccable execution to consistently outperform.

Contents

PART ONE	1
1. A call to action	2
2. What does innovation mean?	6
3. Impact of technology	15
4. Net zero context	30
5. Learn from the best	39
6. Innovation is integral to the vision	53
PART TWO	63
7. Investment thesis	64
8. Innovation portfolio	78
9. Hackathons	93
10. Accelerators	106
11. Corporate venturing	123
12. Winning ideas	142
13. Implementation planning	161
14. People and culture	170

15. Government research and collaboration	182
PART THREE	199
16. Ambitious goals, outstanding implementation	200
17. Making it stick	216
About the Authors	234
Lists of figures and tables	237
Acronyms and abbreviations	238
Acknowledgements	240
Bibliography	242
Index	248
Endnotes	250

PART ONE

WHAT IS SUCCESSFUL CORPORATE INNOVATION?

Chapter 1

A CALL TO ACTION

The world's best performing companies compete based on innovation. They craft a vision that contains practical pathways to success by aligning people, processes, and resources to implement at scale. We call this combination of bold ambition and outstanding implementation *Moonshot Applied*. At its core, it is less about creativity and more about resource allocation.

The need for innovation has never been greater, as technology reshapes markets, making it cheaper to develop more sophisticated products and services accessible on a global basis. However, too often, businesses fail because they believe they do not have the resources or time to divert from business as usual. Too often, they prioritise margins over growth.

In **Part One** we examine the 'what' of successful corporate innovation. Innovation is a critical component of business success, yet it is a confusing term that is difficult to understand and replicate. At its simplest, it involves turning an idea into a profitable solution that adds value to the customer. Often the combination of unrelated insights, it can sustain a company's core business, be adjacent to it, or transform it entirely. Exponential technologies are accelerating the pace of change.

So is the move to net zero. Over the coming decades, trillions of dollars will be invested in the net zero transition, leaving no company, sector, or country untouched.

To sustain exceptional innovation at scale, organizations need to learn from outperformers such as venture capitalists, whose business is commercialising start-ups, and technology companies that adapt rapidly to evolving opportunities. They also learn from leading international and domestic peers. Certain internal decisions, such as making the innovation function report to the CEO, have consistently been shown to make a difference, yet it is surprising how infrequently it happens. Finally, they place innovation at the centre of their vision.

Part Two examines the 'how' of successful innovation. The best innovators are five times more likely to develop an investment thesis about the profound changes that exponential technologies and new business models have on their industries. This provides the focus of their innovation efforts. They invest twice as much in transformational innovation, developing a portfolio that has the potential to solve the industry's key challenges.

Leading innovators generate more sales from new products and services. Repeatable processes scale their innovations to the point where they are big enough to contribute to the business overall. Hackathons (where people engage in rapid and collaborative engineering over a relatively short period of time) take ideas and turn them into minimum viable products. Accelerators take minimum viable products and turn them into start-ups. Corporate venturing takes start-ups and invests capital to turn them into scaleups. These processes apply the same ingredients – specific, ambitious goals;

societal benefit; breakthrough technology; and outside competition and collaboration – to different stages in the company lifecycle. Together, they form an innovation flywheel that accelerates as momentum builds.

Underpinning these processes is a toolset for developing and identifying winning ideas, best practice implementation, aligning people and culture, and collaboration with government research. Leading innovators far are more likely to adopt these tools and collaborate externally than their less successful peers.

Figure 1, below, illustrates the Ipsum innovation model which, in the authors' experience and research, captures the five key areas where leading companies focus their innovation efforts.

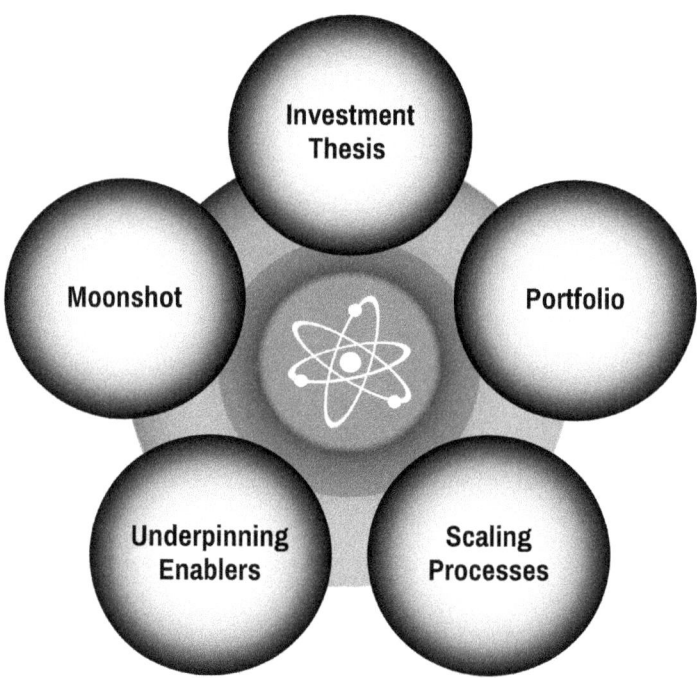

Figure 1. Ipsum innovation model

In **Part Three**, we focus on what to do next. To succeed, businesses need to enhance both their ambitions and their implementation. The Ipsum innovation model details how to do this. The output is a bold innovation aspiration, incorporating key actions to deliver it, appropriate timing, and allocation of the necessary resources.

In summary, *Moonshot Applied* outlines how businesses can learn to spot, develop, and scale exceptional innovations on a repeated basis. It is an optimistic alternative to cost-cutting and price-based competition. Starting with a bold ambition, the best innovators ground their ideas in their unique circumstances. They view themselves, at least partially, as venture capitalists and technology companies. Most importantly, they believe innovation is not a distraction from business as usual; rather, it is the process of defining and creating the company's future.

Chapter 2

WHAT DOES INNOVATION MEAN?

In Part 1, we show the 'what' of successful corporate innovation. Innovation is a critical component of business success, yet it is a confusing term that is often difficult to understand and replicate. At its simplest, it is turning an idea into a profitable solution that adds value to the customer. It is often the combination of seemingly unrelated insights that can sustain a company's core business, be adjacent to it, or transform it entirely. The ability to innovate is now being supercharged by technology, which is improving in an exponential manner, making it cheaper to develop ever-more-sophisticated products and services accessible to users on a global basis.

The best thing since sliced bread

Innovation is about turning an idea into a solution that adds value to the customer. It is rarely the result of a single insight by a lone genius; rather, it is the commercialisation of a combination of seemingly unrelated insights and solutions. For example, Twitch (now owned by Amazon) is a live video streaming service that focuses on video games, including broadcasting esports competitions. When it was spun out of its prior parent company, Twitch disrupted the crowded video streaming market by enabling friends worldwide to watch gaming videos together, live chat about them, and be rewarded by creators for engaging with them. The company took two different but already established technologies – chat and video streaming – and combined them into a single solution, capitalising on the popularity of online gaming.

Twitch is part of a long line of innovations that brought existing technologies together for a new use. The earliest wheel may well have been the potter's wheel, rather than one built for transport. Successful wheeled transport required the development of the axle and the domestication of the horse. The light bulb was demonstrated by Sir Humphry Davy seventy years before Thomas Edison's invention. Edison and his associates worked on at least three thousand different theories before creating an efficient incandescent lamp.[1]
Many inventors had tried making a lightbulb before, but none had found a way to make the light small and weak enough for a residential home. After trying a vast number of different materials for the filament, Edison finally hit on using carbonised cotton thread. However, commercialisation relied on other insights and improvements from the shape and thickness of the glass to the socket for easy replacement and the switch to operate it remotely. Even after he had developed the light bulb, Edison needed ubiquitous electric power to make it a success. He therefore supervised the construction of the first commercial, central electric power station in New York City to help this happen.

At some point, most of us have used (or at least, have heard) the phrase 'the best thing since sliced bread'; however, very few could name when it was invented or by whom. Sliced bread was invented in 1928 by Otto F. Rohwedder.[2] Rohwedder had a degree in optics from the Northern Illinois College of Ophthalmology and Otology. He owned three jewellery stores but was an innovator at heart who developed machines to improve jewellery manufacture before turning his skills to slicing bread. In a remarkable leap of faith, he sold his stores to finance the creation of his prototype sliced bread-making machine. However, it took him a decade to commercialise his invention.

Rohwedder's bread-slicing machine required he solve a number of problems which led to him being granted seven patents. Multiple slices needed to be uniform meaning a special bread-slicing wire, a fast-wrapping process, and a way to place the slices in a cardboard tray, aligning them to allow the machine to wrap the loaf. Loaves were wrapped in wax paper which kept them fresh for longer.

But of course, sliced bread would not be nearly as popular were it not for the toaster. It may be surprising to learn that the toaster was invented before sliced bread. A Scotsman called Alan MacMasters created an electric device he called the Eclipse Toaster. In 1919, the first toaster with a timer and spring was sold commercially as the Toastmaster. So, while we may not know whether the chicken came before the egg, we certainly know that the toaster came before sliced bread.

The 'best thing since...' turns out, like most inventions, to be the result of a combination of seemingly unrelated solutions. Three further insights arise from this case study. Often it takes an outsider to catalyse an innovation. Rohwedder did not come from within the industry but had a degree in optics and ran jewellery stores. The rate of diffusion can be astonishingly fast: only five years after baking industry accepted Rohwedder's machine, 80% of the bread that bakeries in America made were being pre-sliced with it. Finally, successful commercialisation requires deep pockets. To maximise his chances of success, Rohwedder sold his patents to the Micro-Westco Co. of Bettendorf, Iowa, and joined the company as vice-president and sales manager of the Rohwedder Bakery Machine Division.

Types

Innovation can be classified in many ways. However, three primary types of innovation are product, process, and business model. Each plays a distinct role in driving business growth and success. When most of us think about innovation in business, we think about a new product offering. *Product innovation* is developing a new product or improving an existing one to solve a problem in an unexpected or unique way. This type of innovation is often driven by technological advancements, changes in customer requirements and improved designs. Extensive research is crucial in identifying opportunities. Successful product innovation is mutually beneficial for the business and consumer, driving sales and revenue for the company.

Process innovation focuses on improving the practices involved in creating, delivering, and supporting a product or service. This type of innovation can reduce production costs, translating into increased profits. Examples of process innovation include automation of previously manual processes to become more efficient, better forecasting and transparency to make the supply chain more predictable, and eliminating non value-added steps and checks to reduce redundancies.

Business model innovation involves changing the way a product or service is brought to the market. This type of innovation changes the value that is provided to customers and how that value is delivered to generate profit. While the upside of business model innovation is significant, many attempts fail. Successful exponents of this type of innovation include companies such as Dell and Amazon (which cut out distributors by going directly to customers) as well as Airbnb (which created a marketplace where one did not exist before). Successful business model innovation can have a lasting impact on an organisation.

Just as successful innovations combine seemingly unrelated insights and solutions, so too successful start-ups and corporate internal start-ups often require more than one type of innovation to succeed. Who Gives a Crap is an Australian-based social enterprise that sells ethically made toilet paper. It started with a crowdfunding campaign and introduced several innovations into a market that had not changed for decades. The product is made from 100% recycled paper with no dyes (*product* and *process innovation*). The enterprise sells direct to consumers, when toilet paper has previously been bought through supermarkets (*business model innovation*). It is a social enterprise appealing to changes in consumer behaviour that is seeking greater sustainability and community impact, giving 50% of their profits to help improve sanitation in the developing world (*business model innovation*). Finally, the larrikin name and branding positions them very differently from the traditional players in the market.

Taxonomies

Innovation can also be classified according to how it will impact the company and its customers. An important dimension we use throughout this book is whether the innovations will sustain the current core business, develop adjacencies or be transformative.[3] *Sustaining* or *incremental innovation* is the most common type and is based on existing products/services as well as processes. An automotive company puts collision avoidance on a cheaper model of car. A previously manual process is automated. These will typically be implemented in less than a year.

Adjacent innovations are new products or services developed for existing customers who the company understands well, or existing products or services launched in new markets. These can take years to reach scale. An insurance company moves from selling insurance in Australia to selling it to New Zealand. A resources company begins mining a different ore. An automotive manufacturer moves from cars to vans.

Transformative innovation is the introduction of something new that creates significant and lasting change. Amazon's development of the cloud computing provider, AWS, is a good example. Closer to home, Cochlear's first hearing implant is another.

On holiday in 1977, Professor Graeme Clark, an ear surgeon, was fiddling with a shell and a blade of grass when he realised there was a safe way to insert electrodes into the inner ear, rather than have a normal hearing aid. Cochlear was the first organisation to have a multichannel implant approved by the US Food and Drug Administration. Transformative innovations can take decades to reach maturity.

Figure 2, below, illustrates the three types of innovation as they relate to the development of products and services (horizontal access) and the types of customers they are targeting (vertical axis).

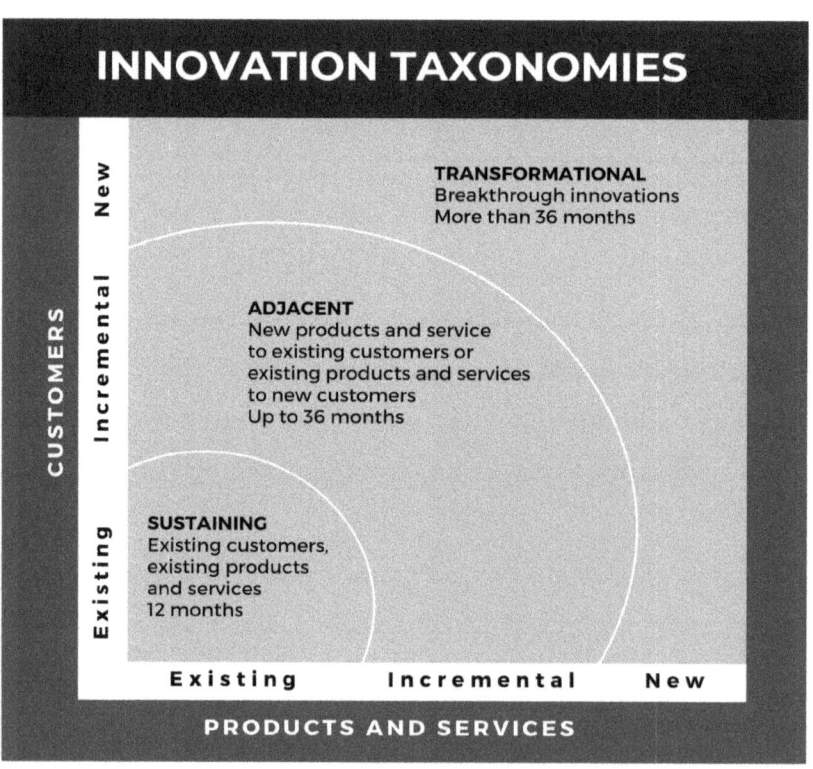

Figure 2. Sustaining Vs Transformational

Technology and innovation

> Nowadays, ideas can meet and mate very much faster than before, and the Internet is only accelerating this process. So, innovation is bound to accelerate.
>
> Matt Ridley, The Rational Optimist

We finish this chapter with a nod to technology and its impact on innovation. Technologies are improving in an exponential manner, making it cheaper to develop ever more sophisticated products and services accessible to users on a global basis.

In the 1930s, American aeronautical engineer, Theodore Paul Wright, published an important paper with a rather dry title, *Factors affecting the costs of airplanes*. In it, he demonstrated that the cost of manufacture declined with experience. Specifically, a doubling of aeroplane production led to a 10–15% reduction in labour costs. This improvement is known as Wright's Law or the Experience Curve. Of course, improvement does not simply need to apply to costs, but can also apply to quality and features. A television today is not only vastly cheaper than a television from twenty-five years ago, but it is infinitely better on every other dimension as well; for example, size, weight, functionality, sound, and picture quality.

The performance of products and services improves with production experience in a predicable fashion. However, the level of improvement is often difficult for us to grasp over the long term because it is exponential. The human brain is accustomed to understanding linear processes. We think about the distance covered by a car at a constant speed or how much someone gets paid per year and what this means to their pay cheque every fortnight. Exponential is different because the improvement compounds. The most well-known example of exponential technology improvement is Moore's Law. Intel's co-founder Gordon Moore declared that the number of transistors in a dense integrated circuit doubles about every two years. In 1975, a 6502 microprocessor had 3,510 transistors. By 2018, the Apple A12X Bionic (ARM64) processor had 10 billion transistors. Pretty much in line with his prediction, but almost incomprehensible at the same time.

Companies looking to drive innovation need to understand the impact of these technologies and why cognitive biases make us discount their impact. Capitalising on them can result in extraordinary opportunities: in a decade, Amazon Web Services (AWS) has grown from $3 billion in revenue to over $80 billion.

Chapter 3

IMPACT OF TECHNOLOGY

Exponential technologies are accelerating the pace of change and businesses harnessing these technologies can deliver significant growth. Where technology innovation involves a software business model, it has the added benefit of being able to deliver outsized returns for shareholders because the bottom line (i.e. profit) can grow faster than the top (i.e. sales)

Exponential

> We tend to overestimate the effect of a technology in the short run and underestimate the effect in the long run.
> Amara's Law

Exponential is a difficult term to understand, so it is worthwhile using an analogy from Ray Kurtzweil, inventor, futurist, and Director of Engineering at Google. If we took thirty linear steps, we would end up thirty metres from where we started and be able to look round to see the spot where we began our journey. However, if we took thirty exponential steps (that is, doubling the distance covered every step), we would end up having travelled over five hundred million metres away, or thirteen times around the planet.

Certain technologies follow an exponential rate of improvement, and as discussed earlier, the most famous of these is semiconductors. In 1965, Intel's co-founder Gordon Moore declared that the number of transistors in a dense integrated circuit doubles about every two years. Moore's Law is a variation of Wright's Law. Moore's Law is a projection based on gains from experience which has held up astonishingly well. Almost sixty years after it was first formulated, it still holds true despite repeated declarations of its death. (As an aside, the death of Moore's Law has been predicted so often that a vice president of Microsoft declared that the number of people predicting the death of Moore's Law doubles every two years.)

Moore's Law is not the only law of exponential technology. Nielsen's Law of Internet Bandwidth states that a high-end user's connection speed grows by 50% per year. This means it doubles roughly every twenty-one months. And Metcalfe's Law states the value of a telecommunications network is proportional to the square of the number of connected users of the system. When Apple released the App Store, it was against received wisdom to bring competitors into the company's ecosystem. However, the large user base it created ensured that popular apps diffused quickly by word of mouth with limited marketing investment. It also made Apple's products more popular with consumers. The freemium business model has evolved to take advantage of these network effects by releasing a free version that will maximise users and then charge a small number of those users for premium features as the primary source of revenue.

Computing cost and power has followed a consistent pattern of exponential improvement for more than fifty years. The impact can be illustrated by the oft-repeated observation that the average smart phone has more computing power than the guidance computer NASA used for the Apollo Eleven mission. In fact, the truth is even more startling. The Apollo Eleven mission was in 1969, but today's smart phone is about five thousand times faster than the CRAY-2, the most powerful supercomputer in 1985!

If Moore's Law is about computer cost and power, Nielsen's law predicts the diffusion of technology which enables computing to be accessed faster and more broadly. In 2005, 16% of the world's population had access to the internet. By 2021, it had grown by a factor of four. Nielsen's law tells us is that what is meant by internet access is improving exponentially. What was a high-end user's connection speed one year will become what an average user's connection speed is in subsequent years.

Computer costs reduce and power increases exponentially. Average internet connection speed grows in a similar manner. The net effect of both is that it becomes cheaper and cheaper to develop ever-more sophisticated, technology-enabled products and services that are accessible to users on a global basis. As we write this book, similar exponential improvements are occurring in artificial intelligence called scaling laws. It is unsurprising that rather than innovation peaking, commentators are talking about a blurring of the boundaries between the physical, digital, and biological worlds.

Klaus Schwab, founder of the World Economic Forum, has dubbed it the Fourth Industrial Revolution.

> The changes are so profound that, from the perspective of human history, there has never been a time of greater promise or potential peril.[4]
> Klaus Schwab, The Fourth Industrial Revolution

Open versus proprietary

Getting exponential technology to scale often requires standards to drive costs down and users up. Standards can be open or proprietary. For example, open-source software makes code available to users to facilitate sharing and modification. Proprietary software prevents users from making changes, publishing new versions, or making copies. Standards are often proprietary in the early stages of the development of many technologies. While proprietary standards may lock out competitors, they also create significant opportunities for an open-source response.

Google is a great example of a company that has used open source to create massive technology markets for itself. When Apple launched the iPhone, Google accelerated its development of Android.[5] Android is a mobile operating system based on the open-source operating system, Linux. Where Apple offered mobile carriers exclusive deals to market its handsets that used a proprietary ecosystem, Google offered open-source Android to every other handset maker and carrier on the promise of providing a flexible, upgradeable, and open system. Being open - source meant a whole ecosystem worked to counter the threat of the iPhone.

> So let me get this straight. You want [Google] to build an external version of the task scheduler. One of our most important competitive advantages. The one we don't even talk about externally. And, on top of that, you want to open-source it?
>
> Googler Tweet

Almost a decade later, Google did the same thing in software automation.[6] Kubernetes (originating from the Greek meaning 'helmsman' or 'pilot') is an open-source system for automating software deployment, scaling, and management. To demonstrate its commitment to open-source, Google offered Kubernetes as a seed technology in the Cloud Native Computing Foundation (managed by Linux). In deciding to go open-source, Google found it received instantaneous feedback from the hundreds of engineers who benefited from deploying it. This created a virtuous cycle where the work of talented engineers led to more interest, which further increased the rate of improvement and usage. The other benefit was that it provided a counter to Amazon's AWS. This meant that thousands of developers had an open-source alternative to AWS which tied them to Google.

A year after its launch, AWS announced support for Kubernetes, effectively acknowledging that it was now a permanent part of the cloud ecosystem.

Interestingly, a focus on open-source has been one of the more important developments at Microsoft since the current CEO, Satya Nadella, was appointed in 2014. Microsoft is currently one of the biggest open-source contributors in the world.

From abundance to wealth

Futurist Peter Diamandis has outlined the pattern of development from an exponential technology to a scalable business model. Products that were previously physical have become digital (for example, photographs). Because they are free, they eat into the existing market. The original product (for example, the camera) is then incorporated into an existing technology (for example, the smart phone) and the cost drops, making the products available to everyone.

Several decades ago, there was a view that the abundance of technology would reduce barriers to entry and make markets more competitive. What is curious about technology abundance is how it has thrown up global players with extraordinarily high market shares – Google in search, Facebook in social media, Apple in smart phones. Successful innovators benefit from network effects, giving them significant barriers to entry. Competitors with a slightly lower market share suffer dramatically from this same effect.

Software is eating the world

More than a decade ago, Marc Andreessen of venture capital firm Andreessen Horowitz published an essay entitled *Why Software is Eating the World*.[7] In it, he argued that 'six decades into the computer revolution, four since the invention of the microprocessor, and two into the rise of the modern internet, all of the technology required to transform industries through software finally works and can be widely delivered at global scale.'

Andreesen looked at Amazon attacking Walmart, PayPal disintermediating traditional banking, and Netflix competing against video stores such Blockbuster. In each case, a software-based business model was eating into a traditional industry. In each case, value was shifting from what was seen earlier as a real or physical supply chain to a virtual one controlled by software. He gives the example of cars and shows how software runs the engines, controls the safety features, entertains the passengers, and guides drivers to their destinations. Presciently, he even observes the move to electric vehicles will only accelerate the value shift.

More than a decade later, this trend continues at an exponential pace and new technologies, not mentioned in his original essay, are building on the old. This includes large-scale machine-to-machine communication, pharmaceutical innovation based on DNA sequencing, and the internet of things.

These technologies are resulting in increasing automation, improving communication and self-monitoring, and smart machines that can analyse and diagnose issues without the need for human intervention. Exponential improvement means an increasing rate of innovation and disruption.

Data

The ability to store, transport and process large amounts of data requires software that did not exist a decade ago. It also means companies have new opportunities to innovate. Data and the ability to process data are now core components of innovation.

Software generates a vast amount of data, which means companies need to invest in data analytics and other capabilities to process it. The Human Genome Project took thirteen years and almost $3 billion to map the human genome.[8] It is now available commercially for $200. The entire human genome requires three gigabytes of computer data storage space. (One million base pairs of sequence data equals one megabyte of storage space; the human genome has three billion base pairs.) The big promise of genome sequencing is to facilitate the analysis of millions of samples to create individual diagnoses or a scale that was unimaginable a generation ago. This same pattern is repeated as thousands of businesses generate billions of interactions with customers and suppliers.

> In our deeply connected world, every interaction produces data and data-driven innovation. Through our global platform, we can create deep connections with millions of small businesses and their advisors. We can leverage the collective power of these connections to open up opportunities to small businesses, which have in the past only been available to large businesses.[9]
>
> Xero's Chief Product Officer

Implications

There is a long-term trend for value to shift from physical products and services to virtual ones managed by software. As successful waves of technology-led change continue, instead of leaving software to the technology giants, companies need to use innovation to find ways to harness it to solve customer problems and benefit themselves. In other words, every large company needs to think of itself as, to some extent, a technology or technology-enabled company. SEEK (Australian leader in online employment marketplaces) will not develop its own artificial intelligence (AI) from scratch but take its unique data set and look to harness AI in innovative ways.

There was a time when the primary role of managers was to manage. Technology was the responsibility of the IT department, a cost centre, rather than a source of competitive advantage. Yet the changes identified in Andreessen's essay and continued in the Fourth

Industrial Revolution are so profound that that thinking is no longer possible.

Today, suppliers disintermediate traditional customer relationships via software. Often, they have lower cost structures and better data insights into customer behaviour than their traditional competitors. For anyone who does not believe this, we recommend *Everybody Lies: What the Internet Can Tell Us About Who We Really Are* by Seth Stephens-Davidowitz (2018). The author is an economist and former Google data scientist. In his book, he shows how time and again Google searches reveal more about what users really think than what they are prepared to say to market researchers, pollsters, or even in customer surveys.

Software continues to eat the world, including older versions of software, causing one wit to write a follow-up to *Software is Eating the World* entitled *Software is Eating the Software that is Eating the World*. Let's take the example of AI. The global AI market value is on track to hit $400 billion by 2027. To understand the rate of change, it is worthwhile looking at board games. In the 1980s, chess world champion Garry Kasparov made a claim that AI could never defeat top-level grandmasters. He successfully defended his title against IBM's Deep Blue in 1996 but was defeated the next year. Less than a decade later, AlphaGo (owned by Alphabet) had taught itself to beat world champions at Go, and it is difficult to see a human beating AlphaGo in a competition ever again.

Where highly complex, specialist tasks like chess and Go lead, others follow. AI software is already used far more widely than most realise.

It is already used in retail, shopping, fashion security, surveillance, sports analytics, manufacturing, and production.

Australian petroleum exploration and production company, Woodside Energy, had no systematic way to tap into the thirty years of engineering and drilling knowledge that lay buried in unstructured documentation and with its most experienced engineers. It therefore harnessed IBM's artificial intelligence platform (Watson) to extract meaningful insights from the equivalent of six hundred thousand A4 pages of data on complex projects.[10] This is particularly the case with shutdown processes, which are irregular and expensive, and therefore often managed by engineers who have never done one before. Using Watson meant harnessing the experience and lessons from previous shutdowns to improve outcomes and safety.

Across multiple sectors, AI is improving the productivity of knowledge workers. In the software industry, it is used to write basic code allowing coders to focus on more specialist development areas. In a study published by GitHub (a US internet hosting service for software development owned by Microsoft), software engineers completed a coding task in less than half the time with the company's AI coding assistant Copilot.[11] Pretty soon, like electricity, it will be hard to imagine, let alone live in, a world without AI.

The response from companies cannot be to leave software to technology giants like Alphabet, Amazon, Microsoft, and Apple because it risks consigning the organisation to irrelevance. Instead, it is about accepting this significant shift in market dynamics and analysing the opportunities to leverage it in their own business.

Mercedes-Benz have an app called *Mercedes me* which promises to unlock the full potential of the vehicle. It allows the owner to remotely control the car – closing windows if rain threatens or turning on the air conditioning so the car is cool when you climb in. The app can be used to search and send a destination, so the car is prepped before you start your journey, and it can locate the vehicle in case of theft.

Cochlear's implants are the global gold standard for the rehabilitation of hearing loss. Since initial commercial release in 1984, over eight hundred thousand cochlear implant surgeries have been performed worldwide. Its innovation history is deeply rooted in the implant, processor, and electrode-side of the business. However, it has also innovated with a software product called *Connected Care* linking the surgical suite to the clinic and into the patient's everyday life.

Yum China (a fast-food business which owns brands like KFC, Taco Bell, and Pizza Hut) was early to embrace digitalisation. As early as 2014, it launched a digital loyalty program which has grown to over four hundred million members by end of last year. Most customers now place their orders through the proprietary apps and digital channels. A senior-friendly app enlarges the fonts and streamlines functions. By utilising AI, it generates recommendations according to user habits and simplifies the purchasing process.

Returning to Woodside Energy, we find it combining the industrial internet of things, AI, edge computing and advanced robotics to deliver timely insights to remote workforces. The deployment of hundreds of smart sensors at the effluent treatment plant at Pluto has trialled the ability to constantly monitor and relay a variety of real-time data about plant performance. The need for a tool to visualise the data has led to the creation of a 4D 'digital twin', which is a spatially referenced virtual replica of Woodside Energy facilities with embedded real-time data analytics. Operators can sense conditions in the effluent treatment plant by accessing real-time data from all relevant sources and can be given insights on what the data means.

> What's empowering is that now you can really reach around the globe in ways where you don't have to create the technology yourself. That is providing anyone with a lot of reach and people can now build mass audiences from anywhere, and I think the monetization layers are going to follow that.[12]
> Bill Tai, legendary Venture Capitalist, Athlete and Adjunct Professor

Business models

When it comes to innovation, most companies focus on the product or service they are planning to produce and spend less time on the business model. A business model refers to how the product or service is delivered to make a profit and create value. It brings us back to the definition corporate innovation as turning ideas into profitable solutions that add value to customers. A critical decision in the success of Android and Kubernetes was to go open-source. A critical decision for Xero was to be a subscription-based platform hosted in the cloud, rather than selling a software licence like many of its competitors.

Software companies are more highly valued than traditional companies – not just because of their ability to grow. The nature of their products means that at a certain inflection point, their sales grow faster than the costs. In economic terms, they have very low marginal costs; for example, the cost to SEEK of hosting one job advertisement is almost indistinguishable from doing a thousand. This means incremental revenues flow to the bottom line. Very few other business models have this characteristic. Service businesses, such as engineering or consulting firms, are traditionally capped by workhours per employee. And if they do succeed in increasing prices, a proportion of the revenue will inevitably feed through into higher wages or the employees will leave. Retailers face the constraint of fixed cost premises and the cost of goods sold. If they sell products at too high a price, it creates an opportunity for competitors to undercut them. Even other technology businesses, like hardware companies, face the issue of manufacturing, adapting to the standards of different countries, and selling through distributors.

Related to this is software's ability to scale rapidly. Software businesses require little additional infrastructure, can be developed from anywhere and sold directly around the world. It is no wonder that app-related businesses are one of the most common start-ups.

The reason for spelling this out in such detail is because too often the authors find companies do not consider software-centric innovation because they do not see themselves as software businesses. The late Harvard professor, Clayton Christensen, found that traditional companies differed from start-ups in that they used a restrictive definition of core competencies, or what they have done in the past, rather than defining themselves by the problem they are solving for their customers.

In a time of great technology shift, every company therefore needs to think of itself as to some extent a technology company. That means doing the innovation work to discover how they can benefit from these profound changes. When reviewing a portfolio of opportunities, companies need to ask themselves to what extent they can benefit from software business models – just as they need to ask themselves to what extent their existing products or services can be enhanced or replaced by exponentially improving technology.

Chapter 4

NET ZERO CONTEXT

Over the next coming decades, no company, sector, or country will be untouched by the trillions of dollars that will be spent as we move to net zero or carbon neutrality. It therefore forms an important context to any organisation's strategy. Some organisations see innovation as part of their environment, social and governance (ESG) responsibilities. However, it is more than that. Leading companies see net zero as an opportunity to drive shareholder value, and innovation as a means of achieving it.

Bill Gates and climate change

> According to a new U.N. report, the global warming outlook is much worse than originally predicted. Which is pretty bad when they originally predicted it would destroy the planet.
>
> Jay Leno

In 2015, one hundred and ninety six countries signed the Paris Agreement, committing them to cut greenhouse gas emissions to net zero by the middle of this century. The scale of this ambition is astonishing. According to estimates from the Global Carbon Project, human activity is responsible for emitting thirty-six billion metric tons of carbon dioxide (CO_2) into the atmosphere each year. This includes emissions from burning fossil fuels for transportation and electricity, as well from industrial processes such as cement production. CO_2 is not the only greenhouse gas produced by human activity, with methane, nitrous oxide, and fluorinated gases also contributing to global warming.

Bill Gates, the founder and former CEO of Microsoft, has written a book on carbon neutrality or net zero, entitled: *How to Avoid a Climate Disaster: The Solutions We Have and the Breakthroughs We Need* (2021). In it, he outlines a comprehensive plan to achieve carbon neutrality by 2050 and mitigate the worst effects of climate change.

This includes five areas of focus:

1. Making things like plastic and steel, which accounts for 31% of emissions.
2. Plugging in, or electricity, which accounts for 27% of emissions.
3. Growing things for food, which accounts for 19% of emissions.
4. Getting around, or transportation, which accounts for 16% of emissions.
5. Keeping warm and cool, which accounts for 7% of emissions.

Leading companies see net zero as much more than an obligation or cost of doing business. They see it as an opportunity to create shareholder value and shape their innovation strategies accordingly. Let's look at three examples of leading Australian organisations in different sectors: Woolworths Group, BHP, and CBA.

Investment in research and development

Gates suggests we need to invest at least $35 billion per year in clean energy research and development, more than five times the current level of investment. Some estimates suggest that total investment will need to reach $1–2 trillion by 2050.

Woolworths Group (Woolworths), one of Australia's largest supermarket chains, is an example of a large corporation investing in public research and development to help achieve sustainability goals. In 2020, Woolworths announced a partnership with the University of Technology Sydney (UTS) to develop new packaging materials that are more sustainable and environmentally friendly. The partnership focuses on developing new materials that can replace traditional plastic packaging, which is a major source of pollution and waste. The goal is to create packaging materials that are biodegradable, compostable, or recyclable, and that can be used for a range of products, including fresh produce, meat, and bakery items.

It would be easy to dismiss this initiative as an environment, social and governance obligation or cost of doing business. However, when this innovation investment is examined in more detail, it becomes apparent that it is much more than that. First, it will help the company reduce its environmental impact and improve its reputation with consumers who are increasingly concerned about sustainability issues. This will help attract more environmentally conscious customers and retain existing ones, translating into increased sales. Second, it will help Woolworths reduce costs associated with waste management and compliance with environmental regulations. This will improve the company's bottom line. By partnering with a leading university, Woolworths is demonstrating a commitment to sustainability. This will help to position it as a leader in the retail industry and could make it more attractive to investors who are looking for companies that are forward thinking and proactive.

In summary, the development of innovative ways to produce sustainable packaging materials through the partnership with UTS can grow Woolworth's sales, reduce its costs, and demonstrate its commitment to innovation and sustainability.

Investment in electric vehicles and transportation infrastructure

The International Energy Agency (IEA) has estimated that we need to invest around $1.7 trillion in charging infrastructure for electric vehicles by 2030 to achieve our climate goals.

BHP has aligned its investment vehicle, BHP Ventures, to support technologies that can help the company achieve its goal of net zero emissions by 2050. The investment vehicle focuses on early-stage companies that are developing innovative technologies in areas such as decarbonisation, electrification, and automation. For example, it has invested in Carbon Clean Solutions, a company that is developing carbon capture and utilisation technologies. BHP is also investing in initiatives to develop green hydrogen, which could be used to power mining operations and reduce reliance on fossil fuels. Its investments even include a company that is developing hydrogen-electric aviation technology that could be used to power BHP's air transportation needs.

It would be easy to dismiss this commitment as virtue signalling. However, in the face of the profound change required to achieve net zero, the scale of BHP's efforts suggests it is looking to find new sources of competitive advantage.

Investment in sustainable agriculture

In 2020, CBA announced a partnership with the Commonwealth Scientific and Industrial Research Organisation (CSIRO), Australia's national science agency, to develop new technologies to support the transition to a low-carbon economy.

The partnership focuses on several key areas, including:

- Clean energy: CBA and CSIRO are working together to develop new technologies to support the transition to renewable energy, such as the integration of solar and wind power into the electricity grid. They are also exploring new ways to store energy from renewable sources, including batteries and other energy storage technologies.

- Sustainable agriculture: The partnership is exploring ways to improve the sustainability of agriculture using new technologies and practices. This includes developing new methods to reduce greenhouse gas emissions from farming, as well as improving soil health and water management.

- Waste reduction: CBA and CSIRO are also working together to develop new technologies to reduce waste and improve resource efficiency. This includes new recycling technologies.

Banks such as CBA understand the risks associated with climate change and need to ensure their investments align with the Paris Agreement goals. The transition to net-zero emissions requires significant investments, and the banking industry will have a critical role to play in financing the transition. Therefore, by adapting to these changes CBA is not only contributing to a more sustainable future but also positioning itself as a leader in the emerging sustainable finance sector.

Cost of doing business or long-term opportunity?

The term environment, social and governance (ESG) was first used less than twenty years ago in a report entitled *Who Cares Wins*, a joint initiative of financial institutions at the invitation of United Nations. Since then, it has grown into a global phenomenon representing more than $30 trillion in assets under management. However, one of the more widely read academic papers published last year argues that we have reached the *End of ESG*.[13]

> [ESG is] extremely important because it's critical to long-term value... Thus, ESG doesn't need a specialized term, as that implies it's niche – considering long-term factors isn't ESG investing; it's investing. It's nothing special since it's no better or worse than other intangible assets that create long-term financial and social returns, such as management quality, corporate culture, and innovative capability. Companies shouldn't be praised more for improving their ESG performance than these other intangibles; investor engagement on ESG factors shouldn't be put on a pedestal compared to engagement on other value drivers. We want great companies, not just companies that are great at ESG.

The reason for spelling this out in detail is twofold: many of the largest companies interviewed for this book have viewed innovation through the ESG lens. Second, the opportunity for companies as we move to carbon neutrality is staggering. Leading companies (such as Woolworths, BHP, and CBA) do not see net zero as just the cost of doing business, but as a long-term opportunity to create value for their shareholders. The way to achieve this is through innovation.

Implications

The authors recognise that there is a balance to be struck between long profitability and short-term investment, but net zero provides an urgent context for a company's innovation strategy. Companies that are seen as leaders in this space benefit from enhanced reputation and brand image. Consumers and investors are increasingly interested in environmental sustainability, and companies that are seen as taking a proactive approach to tackling climate change are likely to be viewed more favourably.

Developing and scaling innovative solutions that reduce carbon emissions and help to slow or reverse global warming can have a significant positive impact on the environment and the planet. Not only is it the right thing to do, but the trillions of dollars of investment required on a global basis represents a major opportunity. The transition to a low carbon economy will bring significant economic benefits, such as the creation of new jobs and industries, reduced dependence on fossil fuels and increased energy efficiency. Companies that can develop and commercialise innovative solutions for carbon reduction are likely to be more competitive in the long term. Innovation can help companies to reduce costs, increase efficiency and meet changing consumer preferences and regulatory requirements.

Referring to Alex Edmand's *End of ESG*, the global goal to achieve net zero will transform every business sector in every country of the world. Incorporating this into a company's long-term planning around innovation is not just the right thing to do, it is the right thing to drive shareholder value.

Chapter 5

LEARN FROM THE BEST

While Australia has world-leading companies and a history of developing innovations, its track record of corporate innovation is poor. Two areas have bucked this trend: venture capital and technology. To be successful, corporate Australia needs to learn what they are doing differently. We also need to learn from the best corporate innovators worldwide.

Innovative companies post higher future profits and stock returns, yet a recent study paints a gloomy picture of the way most businesses consider their future. 56% say advancements in technology are happening at a rate they cannot keep up with. 72% say their executive team lacks the agility to deal with change; 83% find their board of directors often impedes the process.

This book is about how companies can sustain exceptional innovation. As any recovering addict knows, the first step to lasting change is to recognise the problem.

Poor innovation track record

For half a century, Australia has grown its gross domestic product more than double that of Europe. However, its productivity is not great. When it comes to working smarter, Australia's productivity is middling. It ranks eighteenth globally for innovation (according to the OECD[14]) and New Zealand is not much better. The odd thing about this is that in many respects, Australia is a nation of inventors. Australian innovations include the electronic pacemaker (1926), the black box flight recorder (1958), ultrasound (1961), multichannel Cochlear implants (1970s), the polymer banknote (1988), Wi-Fi (1990s), Google Maps (2003) and a cervical cancer vaccine (2006).

No matter what country they come from, mature companies attempting to grow by innovation fail far more often than not. However, as documented by the Business Council of Australia and the Commonwealth Scientific and Industrial Research Organisation, the situation is worse in Australia, where an increasingly risk-averse culture is creating a growing innovation gap with emerging economies. Of course, both Australia and New Zealand have examples of world-leading innovative companies as well as world-leading inventions. There are just too few of them. In general, domestic businesses are not turning research into value. They are not turning R into D.

Venture capital outperformance

Two bright spots have demonstrated the ability to commercialise innovation in spades: private equity/venture capital and technology. (Private equity traditionally refers to investments in later-stage companies, whereas venture capital refers to investment in early-stage businesses, but we will use the terms interchangeably.) Since the 1990s, Australian venture capital has invested $47 billion into Australian businesses. During that time, it has delivered double digit growth net of fees to its investors, a robust outperformance over the listed markets. However, investment in start-ups is still small as a percentage of GDP or per capita relative to other countries.

Large organisations can and need to learn from these organisations that successfully fund start-ups that successfully commercialise ideas. To do so, they must change both their mindset and approach to innovation. Venture capital has small teams who invest in a portfolio of businesses with little or no synergy between them. They manage them on a stand-alone basis. They do not have core competencies as the more traditional company would define them and they accept a far higher failure rate than most traditional companies.

A study of over twenty thousand venture capital investments showed that 65% returned less than the capital invested in them, and 1% earn more than twenty times returns.[15] In other words, failed investments across a portfolio are less important than one might think. What really counts are those with extraordinary returns. This is because investments in innovations are options that give the investor the right, but not the obligation, to invest at a future date. In other words, risk is not symmetrical: the downside is capped, whereas the upside is almost unlimited.

Standard corporate investment does not work like this. It seeks to minimise risk and invest within defined 'strategic' areas of the company's core competence. The figure below illustrates these returns, where zero represent a return equal to the investment. Most organisations would reject a business case with a 65% probability of not returning the investment, let alone create a portfolio of such opportunities. However, this thinking represents a failure to understand the nature of risk: both the risk of investing in innovation and the belief that a company's core business is more stable (and therefore less risky) than history would suggest.

Figure 3, below, illustrates venture capital return on investment risk asymmetry. The vertical axis shows the return on investment where -1 is losing the entire investment and 0 is a return equal to the investment. The horizontal axis is twenty thousand investments in the study.

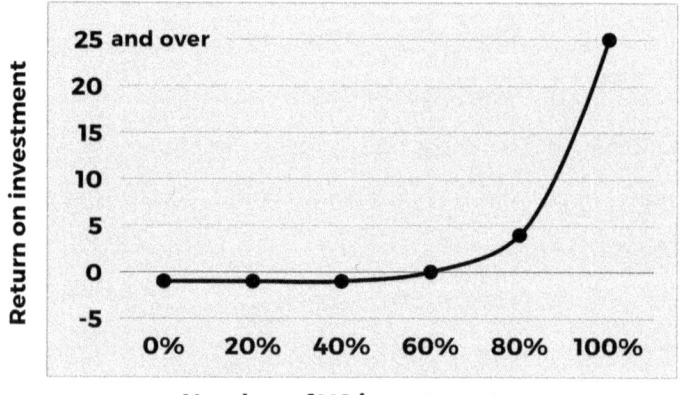

Figure 3. Venture capital return on investment risk asymmetry

A second difference is that venture capitalists focus on medium-term timescales (seven to ten years) and shorter time periods between funding rounds. Planning for most traditional businesses focuses on the annual budget and the long-term plan (for instance, three to five years). Finally, venture capitalists start with the end in mind and look at the exit as evidence of success. Traditional businesses tend to focus on what can be incrementally achieved from today, and do not consider exiting unless the project is a failure.

Technology company outperformance

The other area of remarkable growth is the technology sector. According to the Technology Council (a body representing the technology businesses in Australia), the 'technology sector's economic contribution has increased by 79% since 2016, outpacing average growth in the economy by more than four times'. This trend is repeated in other counties. Over the past twenty years, the NASDAQ (a US share market index heavily weighted toward information technology stocks) delivered returns of over 400%, whereas the S&P500 (an index tracking larger more traditional companies) has delivered 220%. This return includes the recent collapse in technology valuations.

Technology companies grow faster. They tend to be newer, leading to a greater sense of urgency. They are inclined to be less focused on the existing way of doing things and more on solving customer problems, both current and emerging. Therefore, their mindset and processes are more aligned to innovation. Jeff Bezos at Amazon encapsulated this sense of urgency when he wrote: 'Day two is stasis. Followed by irrelevance. Followed by excruciating, painful decline. Followed by death. And that is why it is always Day one.'

Traditional companies need to look at the sector and ask themselves what they can learn from it and how they can participate in it. Two examples show what we mean. The Australian video streaming service, Stan, is an unlikely success story. Launched as a joint venture between local 'old world' media companies, Nine Entertainment and Fairfax Media, Stan faced stiff competition. Netflix had already launched in Australia, bringing with it international content, significant brand awareness (it was already operating in fifty countries) and a well-developed content management platform. Foxtel was a significant local incumbent with almost three million subscribers. Foxtel was also working with another free-to-air broadcaster on a competitor named Presto. Despite this, Nine and Fairfax perceived a gap in the market for on-demand local content other than sports. Stan therefore focused on product innovation by buying international rights mixed with domestic content from its owners.

An important decision for Stan was to launch its own platform rather than set itself up as a channel on a competitor's platforms. This required investment in systems to access and pay for content, manage the film rights, and pay royalties to the artists, directors, and producers. It was a bold decision because it meant embracing new technology rather than leaving it to others. At the end of 2015, the first year in operation, Stan had less than one hundred thousand subscribers.

By 2022, it had revenues of $380 million, making it the largest single domestic streaming service.

A unicorn is a privately held start-up with a valuation of $1 billion or greater. There are currently eight in Australia. One of them, Pet Circle, is an online pet supplies company. Mike Frizell, the founder, noticed one day that his dad was not able to lift the fifteen kilogram bags he normally bought for his golden retriever. He soon realised his dad was not the only one who needed help, and Pet Circle was born. The business then went about building an online software marketplace to engage with consumers directly and backend systems to maximise efficiencies. What is striking about all eight Australian unicorns is that even when they own physical assets, such as physical logistics and warehouses, software is fundamental to their growth and business model. In other words, they are technology-enabled companies.

Given technological disruption and the increasing pace of change, companies that want to innovate need to consider themselves technology or technology-enabled businesses. If that seems outlandish, look at how Amazon has changed physical retailing globally, and how Pet Circle has done something similar in Australia for our furry friends. Look at how 'old world' media companies Fairfax and Nine Entertainment ended up boldly using technology to compete with Foxtel.

Lessons from successful corporate innovators

Having looked at what venture capitalists and technology companies do that is different from traditional businesses, it is time to turn our attention to the lessons from leading corporate innovators, both domestic and international.

Separate and funded

Successful organisations put innovation directly under the CEO and treat it as a risk management exercise. This sounds defensive but, as discussed earlier, risk and return in innovation are not the same as investing in new plant and equipment.

> Innovation is an essential part of Rio Tinto's past, present and future. To remain global leaders in resource technology, we must encourage a mindset that is more accepting of the risks that are inherent in trying new things.
>
> Heidi Edwards, General Manager, Rio Tinto

For innovation to flourish, the innovation function must be independent and properly funded. There is a fine balance to be struck because the innovation team must be close enough to the main business to benefit from its resources, but not so close it is crushed by its culture and structures. Organisations are designed to manage and protect existing products leaving limited space to do new things.

Separation from the day to day business and reporting to the CEO is therefore a key to success. So is long-term funding, because too often funding is insufficient or precarious, resulting in a focus on incremental changes and/or cost reduction.

Bold, communicated and well understood

The second success criterion is that innovation must be bold, well understood, and communicated throughout the organisation. Successful large companies repeatedly asking the question 'What business are we in?' and use the questioning to redefine what they offer. Australia's largest telecommunications company, Telstra, has seen huge changes since it was formed in 1901. Over the past decade alone, telecommunication companies, including Telstra, have seen a migration of value to the 'over the top' providers (for example, Alphabet, Facebook/Meta and Netflix). This means they must reinvent themselves or be relegated to being a 'dumb pipe provider'. Telstra's bold purpose is to build a connected future so everyone can thrive. The former CEO, David Thodey, reminds us that this must be constantly reinterpreted to stay relevant:

> An understanding of the organisation's core business is the first critical factor in approaching innovation. Just because something is possible, doesn't mean you should do it. Directors should ... should revisit an organisation's purpose, its vision and its core offering and reflect on how an innovative idea can enhance it.[16]

Leading innovators share a highly a connected employee population because innovation is a combination of two or more things brought together under a new model. The wheel needed both the axle and the domesticated horse. The light bulb required glass blowing, the carbonised cotton filament, the switch and socket. Sliced bread required bread-slicing wire, a fast-wrapping process, and the modern toaster to reach its full potential. Employees may not have the time, connections, or the structure to bring ideas to reality. Companies must therefore find ways to facilitate creativity through connecting their employees with others who might have complementary passions and ideas.

For decades, 3M Corp. has allotted 15% of its employees' time to innovation, which led to the creation of the now-ubiquitous Yellow Sticky Note, among other products. Alphabet has its 20% time rule, which gives employees a day a week to follow their passions. When employees are enabled through a bold aspiration, culture, rewards and connected through internal online communities, they combine ideas and innovate more often.

Alignment

The final area where successful international companies differ from unsuccessful ones is alignment. One of the biggest barriers to innovation is politics and protectionism. This is not to underestimate the challenges required in optimising business as usual alongside developing breakthrough technologies. However, successful companies develop pre-agreed paths, metrics, and decision processes to create clarity for innovators and the rest of the company alike. They also create alignment in other ways.

In the book *Dual Transformation* (2017), the authors talk about the capabilities that link the core business and new growth areas of innovation. These capabilities align old and new giving the company an unfair advantage as it expands through innovation. When Xerox went into document management it relied on its existing brand, R&D, and salesforce to succeed. When Telstra set up its accelerator, Muru-U, in one of its old telecommunication exchanges in Sydney, it made a strong statement that its innovation was linked to, but separate from, the head office in Melbourne. However, it chose Silicon Valley when it set up its venture fund. Multinational mining company BHP located its venture arm there for the same purpose. In 2021, SEEK split a number of its investments in start-ups into a separate fund to help them get the investment and focus they needed to achieve their full potential. The executive teams are separate, though there are some shared services. However, to create alignment there is a crossover at SEEK's board level. The businesses also continue to operate from the same building meaning there is a lot of informal collaboration.

Successful companies constantly review the linkages and separation between innovation and business as usual to ensure both achieve their full potential.

Core competence and risk

Less successful companies tend to look inwards when they innovate, unlike their more successful peers. In 1997, the late Harvard professor Clayton Christensen published a surprising bestseller, *The Innovator's Dilemma: When New Technologies Cause Great Firms to Fail* (1997). Christensen found that when an innovation emerged that improved performance on dimensions that customers historically valued (for example, the capacity and recording density of disk drives), incumbents tended to lead. However, when an innovation emerged that did not improve along this trajectory but introduced new attributes (for example, small, lightweight, rugged), new entrants tended to win out. This pattern was observed across technology generations and product lifecycles. Large incumbents lose market share by providing their customers with what appears to be the highest-value attributes. By contrast, innovators serving low-value customers with poorly developed technologies improve incrementally until the product is good enough to take market share.

It is unusual for a professor to write a bestseller, and one with such a bleak message for incumbents (whose employees were presumably were the main readers). Christensen therefore wrote a second book, *The Innovator's Solution*: *Creating and Sustaining Successful Growth* (2013), where he recommends incumbents learn from the mindsets of their entrepreneurial competitors. The innovator is not bound by what has succeeded in the past because the success of their start-up is based on solving a customer problem in a unique way, rather than doing what they think they are good at.

Win – lose narrative

The current business narrative is often portrayed as a win–lose between start-up and incumbent, disruptor and disrupted, private equity and corporate, profitability and net zero. However, the picture is more nuanced. According to a recent survey, 75% of fintechs said that partnering with a traditional firm was their primary objective. Other industries are the same. However too often, large corporations are unwilling to engage with start-ups. And too often, start-ups are unwilling to share innovation with larger corporations in case their best ideas are stolen or blocked.

The lesson for both sides is that successful innovation is less based on taking market share and more on creating new markets. *Blue Ocean Strategy* (2015) is a popular approach that focuses on this concept, which challenges organisations to think without assumptions and create new markets rather than competing in existing ones. Instead of trying to outperform their rivals, the strategy encourages businesses to shift their focus to untapped market potential and create uncontested market space, referred to as 'blue oceans'. By identifying areas of unmet customer need, businesses can create new products and services that offer unique value propositions. Therefore, win–lose is not the mindset of leading corporate innovators. These organisations believe they can challenge conventional wisdom and create new market spaces.

They know we live in a volatile environment. However, they also know winnings can be shared, and often must be shared to be successful.

Finally, it is worthwhile tying innovation back to shareholder value. A common misconception is that for most organisations, a percentage improvement in margins will drive more value than an equivalent improvement in growth. For most, it is the reverse. This is particularly the case when markets are volatile.

Finance theory tells us the value of an option increases in times of volatility. Traditional discounted cash flow focuses on a single future with no opportunity to change course or learn from mistakes. In contrast, an option gives the owner the right, but not the obligation, to invest and grow at a future date. It means the owner's downside is capped – they can only lose the cost of the option – whereas the upside is almost unlimited. An option also puts a value on learning: the owner can choose a completely different course based on what they have learned and all that is lost is the initial investment. Rather than a binary winning or losing, leading innovators understand they are creating growth options for the future of their business.

> To be an innovator means that, at times, you will disrupt the status quo and challenge orthodoxies to achieve better outcomes. At CSL, we have a history of disrupting the way things are. Equally, we are not afraid to also disrupt ourselves if it means an even better experience or outcome for patients and public health.
>
> CSL 2030 Strategy

Chapter 6

INNOVATION IS INTEGRAL TO THE VISION

Part 1 has looked at the 'what' of successful innovation. Innovation is turning an idea into a profitable solution that adds value to the customer. Often the combination of unrelated insight. Exponential technologies are accelerating the pace of change. So is the move to net zero. Leading innovators learn from outperformers such as venture capitalists, whose business is commercialising start-ups, and technology companies that adapt rapidly to evolving opportunities. They also learn from leading international and domestic peers.

This chapter shows they put innovation at the centre of their vision. Rather than being impractical or misaligned, their definition of innovation contains practical pathways to success including specific, ambitious goals linked to societal benefit applying breakthrough technology selected via competition.

Original Moonshot

> We choose to go to the moon in this decade and do the other things, not because they are easy, but because they are hard.
>
> J. F. Kennedy

John F. Kennedy gave this famous speech on 12 September 1960, at Rice University in Texas. He had been President of the United States for only a year and the country was losing the space race. A perception that only increased when the Russian cosmonaut Yuri Gagarin became the first man in space. What Kennedy needed was a bold goal to unite the country. Getting a man to the Moon was just such a goal. It was the original Moonshot: an ambitious but specific goal with broad societal benefits, applying breakthrough technology, selected via competition with a third party. Sadly, Kennedy did not live to see his Moonshot achieved. However in 1969, Neil Armstrong landed on the Moon and gave his equally famous speech about a small step for a man in line with Kennedy's original timelines. The fact the speech itself is still quoted is a testament to power both of Kennedy's ambition and the ability of his rhetoric to inspire. The last man on the Moon was in 1972, which shows the huge challenges that were overcome.

Landing on the Moon has proven too expensive to repeat since then, but space flight has grown in unpredicted ways and there are now at least seven organisations offering space tourism including Richard

Branson's Virgin Galactic, Elon Musk's SpaceX, and Jeff Bezos' Blue Origin. In a move that shows that truth is stranger than fiction, the original *Star Trek* actor, William Shatner, recently became the oldest person to reach 'the final frontier' at 90 years of age.

From Moonshot to X Prize

Peter Diamandis was only eight years old when Kennedy gave his Moonshot speech, but it stayed with him for the rest of his life. Diamandis was born in New York and is in many respects the architype at applying Moonshots. Peter had an interest in space from an early age. At eight, he gave talks on the subject to his friends and family. By twelve, he had won first place in the Estes Rocket Design Competition for building a launch system able to launch three rockets at the same time. He is the founder the X Prize Foundation, a $10 million competition that initially attracted twenty six teams from seven countries. The winning vehicle, SpaceShipOne, was piloted to space twice within two weeks. It was the world's first non-government piloted spacecraft, an astonishing achievement within a remarkably short timeframe given the billions of dollars that had been thought to be required prior to that.

Since then, the X Prize Foundation has expanded the focus of the X Prize to address areas around net zero and sustainability using the same methodology. What Diamandis has done is industrialise the Moonshot. It is worthwhile unpicking each the elements to understand how they work:

Set a specific, ambitious goal

When Kennedy set the goal of putting a man on the Moon, no one had any idea of how it would be achieved. To give one example of the challenges they faced, at least three different flight approaches were considered before NASA settled on lunar orbit rendezvous. Even then, it took outsiders to overturn NASA's ground rules about how the moon landing was meant to work.

Former Google (now Alphabet) CEO, Larry Page, dubs this setting of ambitious goals as 10X thinking. It means thinking about something that is ten times better than existing options. Our natural way to approach any problem is linear, but technology improves exponentially. An ambitious goal, such as sending a man to the moon within a decade, forces us to attempt innovative approaches to the problem which would not be attempted if we were only aiming at incremental, linear improvement. It makes us think in an exponential manner. Moreover, a 10X improvement does not necessarily require ten times the effort which means it makes sense from a risk/reward basis. On top of this, big goals have the advantage of attracting smart, ambitious people. Finally, it is worthwhile noting the adjective 'specific' is important because it grounds the ambition in something tangible and measurable.

Link it to societal benefit

Kennedy's speech appealed to the pioneering American spirit, the sense of destiny and exceptionalism. However, it did so in the context of creating a better global society: 'We set sail on this new sea because there is new knowledge to be gained, and new rights to be won, and they must be won and used for the progress of all people.' In a similar vein, Diamandis' X Prize is not primarily about becoming rich, but about solving some of society's deepest challenges. Most people want to feel part of something bigger and more meaningful than themselves. Doing something good is a significant motivator providing the fuel to strive harder and a filter to direct efforts.

OpenAI, an organisation that has created a great deal of publicity through its development of ChatGPT, has a mission to 'ensure that artificial general intelligence – by which we mean highly autonomous systems that outperform humans at most economically valuable work – benefits all of humanity.'[17] For businesses, societal benefit is not charity (or not simply charity), it can be quite hard-nosed. The non-profit OpenAI has restructured itself as a for-profit start-up with a non-profit parent. This has enabled it to access the funding it needs to continue developing the platform. Societal benefit is OpenAI's mission, but commercialisation is both an economic necessity and a pathway for its technology to learn about the world.

A good example of how to manage this tension between societal benefit and shareholder value is Australia's GrainCorp, whose investment in innovation is part of its contribution to domestic agriculture. GrainCorp is a one hundred year old, Australian, listed agribusiness with operations spanning four continents. GrainCorp's success measures around innovation are to make Australian agriculture more competitive globally within the context of a net zero future. Australia is a challenging country to farm with volatile weather conditions and varied soil quality, and because of this, Australia has some of the world's best farmers. These farmers compete in a global marketplace where the lowest cost to serve wins. An investment in innovation is part of GrainCorp's contribution to the domestic industry. GrainCorp's success measures are therefore about making Australian agriculture more competitive globally on the hard-nosed assumption that if Australian agriculture does well GrainCorp will do also do well.

Applying breakthrough technology

The original Moonshot necessitated breakthroughs across a range of diverse areas such as nutrition, materials, and textiles. Even today, the NASA's website lists a range of products that have come out of spaceflight from camera phones to memory foam. Innovative companies do not focus on research for its own sake; but rather, like NASA, they focus on solving problems using feasible technology.

Outside competition and collaboration

Finally, there is an element of outside competition and collaboration involving outsiders. Outside competition creates a broader pool of potential solutions than might occur if the company tries to back winners or just use insiders. There is also an urgency that may not be there without the thought that someone might beat you. In the case of Kennedy, the competition was with the Soviet Union. Drilling down into NASA's interaction with outside technology firms, we find a wide variety of partners, from Motorola, Honeywell, General Motors to Pratt and Whitney. We also find a variety of contracting styles from cost plus to fixed price to select the best partners to work with on different components of the project. In the X Prize, teams from around the world compete not just for the prize money, but for the prestige that comes with winning.

During the 1950s, Seiko had a reputation for unreliability, so much so that the watches even stopped working while they were being tested! That changed when Seiko put their own factories in competition with one another to try and beat the Swiss at the own game. Having done that, they took the best ideas and innovations from each factory to become an industry leader. Competitions are even used in creative endeavours. Band/song camps have been around since the early 1990s where musicians are invited to pitch ideas for all or parts of songs in a forthcoming album, knowing they are in competition and their ideas might not be accepted. For Rihanna's album *Rated R*, Antonio 'L.A.' Reid hosted what has been called the mother of all song camps. Sales of the album exceeded three million and band/song camps have only multiplied since then.

Competition need not be 'red in tooth and claw' as Tennyson memorably puts it. The goal is to stimulate and form bonds that create a sense of belonging and camaraderie as individual and teams work together in a common the challenge.

Case study: Google X, the Moonshot factory

In 2010, Google (now Alphabet) founders Larry Page and Sergey Brin formed a new division of the company to work on Moonshots:

radical ideas that made the world a better place. It was a grand experiment – some might say a Moonshot unto itself – and a nod to Peter Diamandis X Prize. Over more than a decade, Google X has incubated hundreds of different Moonshot projects, many of which have gone on to become independent businesses. Each Google X idea adheres to a simple three-part formula. First, it must address a huge problem; second, it must propose a radical solution; third, it must employ a relatively feasible technology.

Has it succeeded? Alphabet does not release Google X's budget or staff numbers. However, Waymo, a self-driving technology company, has graduated from Google X as a separate subsidiary. Analysts have valued the business at $30 billion or 2–3% of Alphabet's market capitalisation. Alphabet is not an automotive company, but it is an artificial intelligence company. A move from artificial intelligence for search, to artificial intelligence for self-driving cars, does not seem too radical when put in the context of Alphabet/Google's mission to organise the world's information and make it universally accessible and useful. Googlers have observed that Waymo's valuation alone far exceeds the cumulative costs of running Google X since its inception.

Applied innovation

Part One has examined the 'what' of successful corporate innovation. A bold vision is important to galvanise an organisation. Innovation must play more than a part. For leaders, it is integral to the whole, or what Dan Ratner, CEO of Uberbrand, calls the zeitgeist: getting to the essence of how a brand stays relevant through its links to a broader change.

Google 'strives for continual innovation, not instant perfection'. Amazon is guided by 'customer obsession rather than competitor focus, passion for invention, commitment to operational excellence, and long-term thinking.' Apple's mission is 'to create technology that empowers people and enriches their lives.' Closer to home, CSL's mission is 'to discover, develop, and deliver innovative therapies that improve patients' quality of life.' In each of these examples, the commitment to innovation is easy to recognise as an integral part of the whole.

Part Two examines the 'how' of innovation and demonstrates the ways in which leading innovators act differently to get exceptional results. We call it the Ipsum innovation model. Innovation leaders develop a thesis about the impact of exponential technologies and new business models on their industries. This provides direction for their investment to turn threats into opportunities. They develop and manage a portfolio of innovations, investing twice as much as their less successful peers in breakthrough ideas. They are better at scaling their innovations through hackathons, accelerators, and corporate venturing, using specific goals, societal benefit, breakthrough technology and collaboration to build momentum. Their innovation processes are more likely to be underpinned by tools for recognising and developing wining ideas, best practice implementation planning, aligning culture and people, and collaborating with government research.

A series of questions at the end of the relevant chapters guides leaders on what they need to consider next. Not all parts will be equally relevant for each company, but by working through the sections they can develop a plan of action to innovate at scale that suits their unique circumstances.

PART TWO

How to apply a Moonshot

Chapter 7
INVESTMENT THESIS

Part Two looks at the 'how' of corporate innovation. Leading innovators excel in five areas and this section provides an approach to learning from them: investment thesis, portfolio management, scaling processes and underpinning enablers. All these feed into the five area, the Moonshot, which is dealt with in Part 3.

This chapter focuses on developing an investment thesis, an area where the company focuses its innovation resources and has advantages which make it likely to succeed. Developing a thesis relies on understanding the strategic goals of the company; mapping the relevant changes in exponential technologies; discovering more about the potential business models and their impact on the market; and articulating where it plans to invest.

Ipsum innovation model

'Ipsum' is Latin for yourself/thyself, as in *Medice, cura te ipsum*, 'Physician, cure thyself' (Luke 4:23). The model summarizes the five key areas where successful innovators differentiate themselves.

IPSUM INNOVATION MODEL

INNOVATION AREA	KEY COMPONENTS
Investment Thesis	• Role of innovation in corporate strategy • Exponential technologies & disruptive business models • Focus & competitive advantage
Portfolio	• Composition & potential
Scaling processes	• Hackathons • Accelerators • Corporate Venturing
Underpinning enablers	• Spot & Develop Winning Ideas • Plan & Manage Implementation • People & Culture • Collaboration with Government research
Moonshot	• Goals • Actions • Timelines • Resources

Table 1. Ipsum innovation model components

Exponential technology is accelerating the pace of change. Ray Kurzweil calls this the Law of Accelerating Returns (a variant of Wright's Law) and observes that it applies across all information technology fuelled by information. Once any domain, discipline, technology, or industry becomes powered by information, the rate of improvement (price and/or performance) begins doubling at regular intervals. This continues for decades. This chapter examines how organisations can explore and respond to these technologies turning threats into opportunities. We call it map, discover, develop.

Despite many companies placing innovation as one of their core values or missions, fewer than 25% of board directors and CEOs are involved in setting innovation targets and budgets. Companies may not succeed in achieving these targets; however, they will certainly fail without them.

Strategic context

> The strategy dimension has got to come first. You innovate within that. If you don't have strategy then you get novelty, inconsistency, incoherence. Innovation is important, but it's dangerous in isolation. If you're innovating in a bubble, you can do more harm than good.
> SEEK co-founder and chief executive, Andrew Bassat

If the company has an explicit innovation strategy setting out where innovation fits into the overall strategy with quantified and funded targets, and there is complete overlap between this and the exponential technologies, then there is no need to read further. If there is a gap, then the company needs to develop an investment thesis similar to the way a venture capitalist describes itself to attract investors and start-ups. The thesis should include the technologies the company will focus on and the 'secret sauce' or unique insights it could expect to bring to make the investment more likely to succeed. We call the process to get there map, discover, develop.

'the dawn may kindle'

In late 2003, Steve Jobs (CEO of Apple) invited Jeff Bezos (CEO of Amazon) to his offices at Cupertino.[18] At the meeting, Jobs gave a demonstration of the soon-to-be-launched iTunes for Windows. He then outlined his views on the potential impact on the music industry, especially CDs, and said that Amazon might well be the last place to buy them because consumers would move online to a cheaper, faster and more flexible experience that is, iTunes. What is interesting is Jeff's Bezos' reaction. What many CEOs would have done was to bring the company together to develop a project to combat this existential threat, create a copycat digital music solution, and issue a press release claiming it would win the day. Instead, Amazon went through a process that led to a completely different outcome.

Bezos took seasoned executives out of their day jobs and put them in charge of developing a response. There was a great deal of pressure to do something quickly. They looked at music, TV, and books. In music, piracy was destroying Amazon's CD business and Apple was rapidly gaining traction selling millions of songs on iTunes to millions of its iPod customers. Music producers alternately goaded and courted Amazon to develop a competing service. When the executives moved from music to TV, they found content creators had no interest in licensing shows or movies to digital service providers. Finally, they turned to e-books, where a small market existed, but publishers were not investing in it, and they only released a small catalogue of e-books at the same high prices as hardcovers.

Amazon considered being a fast follower to Apple and buying existing start-ups with a scalable technology. However, Bezos believed Amazon was an innovator not a fast follower, a company that developed new markets and solutions that in turn delivered better returns to shareholders. The challenge for his team was that while there was a road map to be fast follower, there was no roadmap for innovation. They needed to build the road themselves.

Books were still the single largest category at Amazon. However, the e-book business was tiny, and there was no good way to read books on a device other than a PC, which was a poor experience. Based on the success of iTunes/iPod for music, the company believed that customers might want the e-book equivalent: an app paired with a mobile device that offered consumers any book ever written, at a low price, that they could buy, download, and start reading in seconds.

The next hurdle was how to build such a device because the company had no experience in hardware. Bezos emphasised that Amazon's approach was to start from the customer and work backwards. Figure out what the customer needed and then ask themselves if they had the necessary skills to fulfill those needs and if not, how they might acquire them. They hired a Silicon Valley veteran who had been a vice president of hardware engineering at Palm Computing. He set up a separate office in Silicon Valley. In parallel, two trusted Amazon engineering vice presidents established and hired a software engineering team to build the cloud back-end systems.

The result was Kindle, a portable e-reader that allowed customers to purchase and download books wirelessly from anywhere in the world. Kindle was designed with the customer in mind, offering a superior reading experience with a screen that mimicked the appearance of paper and a long battery life. To create the Kindle, the team had to develop new technologies, such as the electronic ink display and wireless connectivity. Since its launch, Amazon has sold almost half a billion Kindle e-readers representing two-thirds of the market.

Getting down to brass tacks

The approach that Amazon took to developing the Kindle is unlikely to drop out of traditional business planning. Traditional business planning will often use a framework like Michael Porter's Five Forces which includes analysing customers, suppliers, substitutes and rivals. There are several challenges with this approach.

It does not explicitly address exponential technology. It tends to work forwards from the status quo which may underestimate the impact of disruption for example, the massive changes required to meet net zero. This is compounded by a focus on competitive market share rather than the customer's unmet needs which leads to analysing existing markets rather than creating new ones, imitation rather than innovation.

Innovation can disrupt traditional market structures as suppliers cut out the middleman. The Dollar Shave Club launched in 2011 selling directly to end users rather than the traditional method for manufacturers like Gilette and Wilkinson, which sold through retail stores. Add exponential technologies (for example, Amazon's development of Kindle) and the disruption accelerates. It is critical therefore to understand technologies relevant to the company (whether it be e-readers, AI, precision therapies, or green hydrogen) and how any threat posed by them can be turned into an opportunity. Rather than five forces, the authors prefer a simple, specific approach that involves:

- mapping the exponential technologies relevant to the company

- discovering more about the business models to commercialise these technologies and their impact on the market

- developing an investment thesis about where the company is willing to invest.

Mapping technologies

As discussed earlier, we often struggle to understand the compounding impact of exponential technologies. Several examples from different industries illustrate the point:

- The cost of utility scale solar power has declined sixfold from 2010 to 2020. The US Department of Energy estimates it will be 0.02/kWh by 2030. A fourteen times reduction in twenty years is very predictable when it is understood, but very few power companies would have acted on that insight in 2010!

- According to data from the World Economic Forum, by 2025 robots will perform 52% of human tasks (today, 29% are automated). The Roomba robot vacuum cleaner has made some progress in vacuum cleaning, but what are the other activities that are likely be replaced in the home, and what will be people do with the spare time given the exponential growth in broadband?

- A study by the US firm GitHub found software engineers completed a coding task in less than half the time when they worked with the company's AI coding assistant, Copilot. If this rate of improvement continues, AI coding assistants like Copilot could increase the output of software engineers around tenfold by 2030.

- Cell-based meat is produced in a laboratory/ factory using animal cell culture technology, where meat is produced from animal cells using a combination of biotechnology, tissue engineering, molecular biology, and synthetic processes. Over time, producing a cell-based beef burger has fallen ten thousand-fold from $1 million per kilogram to $100 per kilogram. This cost is expected to fall below $10 per kilogram by 2025. The implications for the beef industry, especially as we move to carbon neutrality, are profound.

There is considerable knowledge and interest about the future within most organisations. There is also a great deal of extant research on most of these topics. While many working in large organisations will not be surprised by exponential technology within their domain, there is often not agreement at executive and board about its impact, let alone the appropriate response. The first step of the diagnostic is therefore to get a common understanding of the potential impact of these changes. Mapping out the exponential development of relevant technologies provides an important input to gauge the urgency with which businesses need to change.

Discovering business models

The next phase is to discover more about the business models used to commercialise these technologies and their impact on the market. The intention is to understand the impact of trends and turn potential threats into opportunities. Business models can change the dynamics in a market. Google and Facebook have advertising-based revenue models that are free to the user. Australian unicorn Canva brought the freemium business model into design and publishing, and only a small number of superusers pay for the service. Netflix and Spotify have replaced one-off transactions through stores with direct consumer subscriptions. Airbnb brought a marketplace business model to accommodation. Shopify has used an affiliate revenue model, which promotes links to relevant products and collects a commission on the sales of those products.

Any business model analysis needs to cover the whole value chain. Warning signs include whether customers are changing their behaviour; whether venture capitalists are becoming more active; and whether new business models are emerging. The trick is to try and look at how the eco-system appears to others. Does your competitive advantage appear as complacency to the company in an adjacent space? Does your customers' satisfaction about what you are providing mask an unmet need?

In the case of Amazon's development of the Kindle, executives discovered more about these changes by attending conferences, talking to music and book publishers, as well as studio executives. However, what really drove Bezos' thinking was the customer. Customers were not unhappy with CDs and cassettes. However, iTunes had shown there was an enormous demand to access online music that was not pirated. Consumers liked it because it was cheaper, more easily accessible than traditional sources, and did not degrade or get damaged. It was also legal and therefore the musicians were paid. However, the whole package had to be a great customer experience to change behaviour which, for Amazon, meant controlling both the hardware and software in a new business model. Innovation did not stop there and Amazon is now investing heavily in audio books expanding the market to cater for customers who prefer to consume this way.

Discovery means moving from understanding the trend to considering its implications. SEEK is aware of the danger of disruptive business models to the extent that it searches out businesses that might disrupt its online employment marketplace, deconstructs their approach, and runs trials in contained areas of its business to understand the potential impact.

Develop an investment thesis

Finally, businesses need to develop a thesis about where they are prepared to invest and what unique advantage they bring to make them more likely to succeed. Leading innovators are five times more likely to have a coherent investment thesis than their less successful peers. The idea for Kindle took place at the end of 2003. Amazon investment thesis focused on music, film, and books, but only in the latter was it convinced it could bring something unique. As the product evolved, Amazon used internal resources and poached hardware talent from other industries. It also acquired a small company based in France that had built a software application for viewing and reading books on PCs and mobile devices. Kindle was launched four years after that initial meeting with Steve Jobs and the first run sold out in less than six hours.

Closer to home, the *Australian Financial Review* publishes an annual list of the most innovative companies. In the financial services category, the winner was Visa's Geospatial Analytics Capability which uses an artificial intelligence model to determine a customer's 'effective area of influence', or the suburbs where they like to shop, and what they like to spend. This information can then be harnessed by tourism providers and local councils to prioritise funding to boost local economies. And one of the runners up was Honey Insurance. For years, health insurers have encouraged people to stay healthier, car insurers have rewarded customers for driving less, so why do home and contents insurers not do the same thing? Honey Insurance's sensors are purpose built to prevent accidents and claims. Placing one near a smoke alarm means homeowners will be alerted if a fire breaks out while they are away. Sensors on doors detect motion in the event of a break-in, and those placed under washing machines detect water leaks. Both Visa and Honey's innovations have come from taking technology outside the core financial service offering and adapting it to provide something new.

Practical, measured steps to reach agreement on the existence of a gap between the threat/opportunity and the status quo comes from looking at the company's current innovation goals and putting them alongside what has been agreed are the exponential technologies and business models that may disrupt the industry. It means identifying and agreeing areas where the organisation is willing to invest and what capabilities give it the right to succeed.

Deciding where to play is essential. The consulting group BCG publishes a list of the world best innovators. What we call an 'investment thesis', BCG calls an 'innovation domain'.[19] Their most recent report concludes that the best innovators focus on a limited number of innovation domains in which they can leverage a unique strategic asset or capability, such as superior customer access, that others cannot match.

This is not easy as many companies struggle to define what makes them special. Søren Kierkegaard reminds us that life must be lived forwards but can only be understood backwards. In successful companies, the unique insights are often self-evident only in retrospect. Apple consistently focuses its innovation efforts on making its products easier to use than its competitors' and providing a seamless experience across its expanding family of devices and services. Its innovation skills centre on integrated hardware–software development, proprietary operating systems, and design. They are not on producing the cheapest product. The growth in the wearables division fits into this thesis. It is also interesting to see that the services division (digital payments, the App Store, on-demand TV streaming, iCloud) represents an increasing component of their revenue and reinforce the existing hardware-software ecosystem.

In the case of Visa, the thesis was about using artificial intelligence and internal data to create a new market. In the case of Honey Insurance, it was enhancing home insurance by investing in smart home products. Atlassian has two innovation processes: an internal one that takes employee's improvement ideas and provides a process and investment to grow them with a target of reaching $100 million in revenues using the Atlassian platform; and an external one that invests in collaboration apps with the potential to be the next big hit on the Atlassian Marketplace. A company like Atlassian is exploring other areas, but this simple statement or thesis provides a framework to channel its innovation investment.

For the former CEO of Fortescue Metals Group (FMG), Andrew Forrest, the investment thesis is around green hydrogen. As part of building the Fortescue Futures Industries business, Forrest's FMG asked it to develop both a hydrogen powered mining haul truck and a blasthole rig. Decarbonising mining fleets is one of the largest challenges facing the Resources industry and to date there are no vehicles that are economically viable. As a key step in FMG's Moonshot to renewable energy, the organisation chose to fund a team with the goal of developing and commercialising such a vehicle.

Key questions

- Does the company have an explicit innovation strategy illustrating where innovation fits into the overall strategy with quantified and funded targets?

- Has it mapped the relevant exponential technologies across the value chain?

- Has it discovered the business models to commercialise these technologies and their potential impact on the market?

- Has it developed a thesis about where the company will focus its investment and the 'secret sauce' or unique insights it could expect to bring to give a higher probability of success?

- Are there gaps between questions above and current strategy?

Chapter 8

INNOVATION PORTFOLIO

Having developed a thesis about the innovation the company will invest in and the 'secret sauce', or unique advantages, it could expect to bring, the next stage is to examine the portfolio. This means defining the current portfolio's composition and potential; establishing whether there is a gap between it and the company's aspirations; and managing the portfolio moving forward. Leading innovators commit twice as much of their innovation budget to transformational innovation when compared to their less successful peers.

Defining the portfolio

At the beginning of this book, we said that innovation is turning an idea into a solution that adds value to the customer. For corporates, we need to add an additional condition, because the goal of any business is to drive wealth for its shareholders. The full definition should therefore read: *an innovation is turning an idea into a profitable solution that adds value to the customer.* While many talk in general terms about the importance of creativity to culture and why innovation fits into a company's environment, social and corporate governance obligations, we are interested in growth in value, being monetary or another form of shareholder benefit. Innovation is therefore a matter of resource allocation. It is about focusing the company's people, assets, capital, and management attention on the impactful ideas which are most likely to deliver meaningful long-term returns.

Having agreed on the potential impact of exponential technologies and decided to act (the 'why'), the next step is to examine the company's current portfolio of innovations. Every company is working on improvements. They may not call them innovations, but it is important to classify appropriate improvements or new solutions into a portfolio then review them in terms of their cost and impact. An innovation portfolio is a collection of research programs, investments, enhancements, new solutions, minimum viable products, and so on, with defined aspirations and required resources. There can be considerable discussion about what constitutes each innovation in the portfolio, so it is worthwhile identifying a few criteria.

- The innovation must be *a new way of doing things that solves an unmet stakeholder need (the 'who').* This differentiates it from business as usual. For example, a company entering a new country defined this project as an innovation because it required a considerable change to its existing products. The same company did not include the addition of a new version of Android functionality to its website because this was seen as business as usual.

- It must be *a defined solution (the 'what') that has received and requires investment (capital and other resources)*. Another business decided to include the development of a range of value priced products into its innovation portfolio, but not a range of recycled packaging. Its logic was that while the packaging was new, it was an enabler to the company's business, rather than a defined solution in its own right.

- It must align *to a business model that allows for the solution to be beneficial or monetised (the 'how')*; that is, it must have the potential to deliver a defined benefit to the company that can be attributable to the innovation. A telecommunication company decided to trial a new transmission technology. It was a new technology that would meet an unmet need and a defined solution with a budget to install and trial it. However, having reviewed the investment the company decided not to include it in its innovation portfolio because the technology was more than five years away from commercialisation and there was no obvious means to monetise it. The investment was therefore justified as a marketing exercise to generate positive publicity. These may be good reasons to make the investment; however, they are not reasons to class it within an innovation portfolio.

We discuss different ways to value an innovation later in the book. At this stage, it is worthwhile pointing out that the simplest way to compare the potential of innovations is to use the revenue they are expected to generate versus the investment.

Thus, if the company wishes to put cost-saving innovations into its portfolio (for example, process automation), it makes sense to tie this back to some type of revenue number (for example, additional revenue if the cost savings were passed onto the customer in terms price reduction or if the saving was spent on additional customer acquisition). Similarly, if ESG or employee satisfaction outcomes are the focus of the innovation, then how do they flow back to improved company profitability.

Defining the portfolio requires discussion and agreement. The three criteria, discussed above, provide a way of thinking about whether innovations fit into the portfolio. A new way of doing things that solves an unmet customer need (the 'who'). A defined solution (the 'what') which has received and requires investment which has the potential to deliver a financial benefit to the company that can be attributable to it (the 'how'). Who-what-how is only an indicative framework. To misquote *Pirates of the Caribbean*, it is more 'what you'd call guidelines than actual rules'.

Evaluating the portfolio

Once the innovations have been defined, the next step is to evaluate them. Every company is different, and leading companies will most likely use an internal template to measure comparability across the portfolio. This will include:

- Short description of the innovation: who-what-how.

- Investment to date and future required investment.

- Business benefit and valuation. This may include broader business benefits if the innovation leads to learning that can be applied to different situations. Management can use their own internal valuations or externally validated ones for example, with a third-party capital raise. It is hard to value very early stage innovations, especially transformative ideas, hence it is important not to slavishly follow financial metrics, but complement them with non-financial ones that place a value on exploration and creating new knowledge.

- Technology readiness level (TRL), or some other form of tracking the maturity of technologies during the development or acquisition process.

- Business plan and milestones.

- Team, capabilities, resource allocation.

- Key portfolio metrics: innovation, type and so on.

Most companies include a risk analysis, but we advise against making too much of this. First, because risk is highly subjective, and a simplistic view of risk leads companies to drop early stage and focus on later stage investments. More importantly, many companies misunderstand the nature of risk. Innovations are options with significant upside and a capped downside. If the very best venture capitalists make their returns from only a tiny proportion of their investments, then risk management is more about the breath of investments and the processes to manage them, rather than deciding top down which have the right to succeed.

The portfolio review example below has been taken from the authors' experience of working with an Australian organisation, but the numbers have been disguised. After much discussion, the company finalised a smallish portfolio of ten innovations representing an investment of around $20 million. All are viewed as likely to deliver a positive return on the current and planned investment. Unlike many organisations, rather than relying on sales, it had performed a valuation on each. The portfolio was heavily skewed with two main innovations representing 70% of the portfolio. These two were large IT projects that were designed to deliver significantly higher sales through reductions in cost and time for the company's core products. As might be expected, these larger, later-stage investments, had a lower return ratio (value divided by investment) than the smaller, more early stage ones.

Looking more closely at the portfolio, most of the investment was going into the commercialisation of these two technologies. While the company believed it did not have the resources to trial many new innovations, it had funded some early stages proof-of-concept ideas for enhanced products on the new platform that it was hopeful would generate returns in the future.

Finally, we looked at whether any of the innovations in the portfolio was transformative, not necessarily in terms of changing every aspect of the business, but in terms of introducing new offers or businesses serving new markets and customer needs.

The key insight for management came when we agreed that all of the investment was going into sustaining the core business. Little was targeted at moving into adjacent markets or customers and none into transformative innovations.

Existing processes were being digitised, systems upgraded and moved to the cloud, and so on These enabled the organisation to deliver more for less and hopefully add capabilities at the same time. There was one innovation that might be classed as adjacent allowing the company to draw on existing capabilities and put them to new uses. This required new insights into customer needs which had not been well thought out. However, as shown in the next diagram, the portfolio was unbalanced because the company's innovation thesis was about achieving longer term thinking in its chosen areas rather than just a focus on delivering the current budget. The size of the circles represents the level of investment in each innovation.

Figure 4, shows the company's portfolio by innovation type with the horizontal axis representing whether the innovation was focused on existing or new products and services and the vertical axis representing whether the innovation was focused on existing or new customers. The size of the bubbles represent the size of investment.

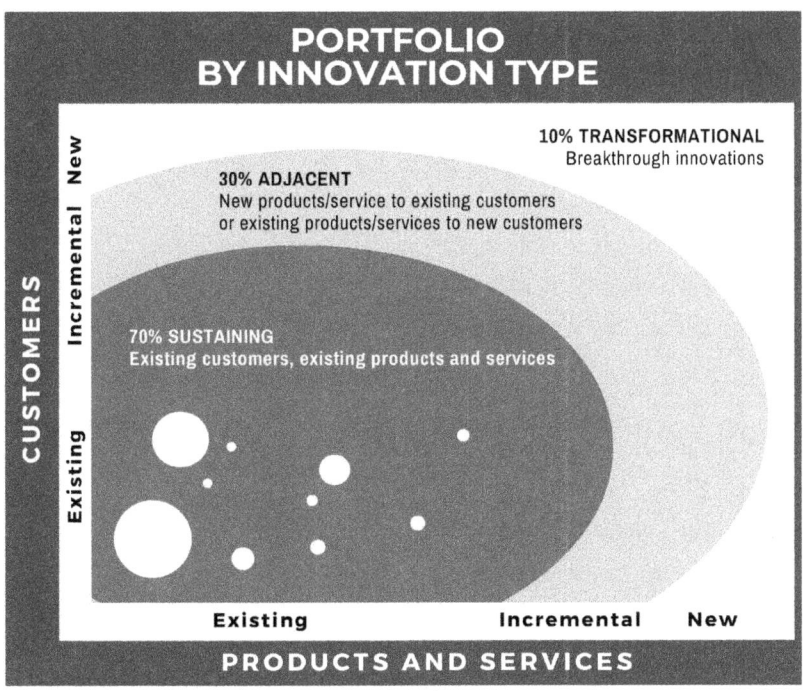

Figure 4. Too little transformation

Golden rule

High-performing firms have been found to allocate 70% of their innovation resources to sustaining innovation, 20% to adjacent innovation, and 10% to transformational innovation. Sustaining refers to innovations that can impact the core business within a year; adjacent, within three years; and transformational, more than three. This golden ratio has been adopted by Google and others.

While the exact ratio differs for different companies and for different stages in the economic cycle, the idea is that part of the budget should be earmarked for transformative innovation, notwithstanding the low likelihood of success, and not diverted because of pressures for short-term financial performance.

The 10% in transformational innovation is more than twice what less successful innovators invest. Companies that adopt it have been found to enjoy a 10–20% premium to their peers. Interestingly, they tend to get the reverse returns ratio on their innovation. Sustaining innovation efforts typically contribute 10% of the long-term, cumulative return on innovation investment; adjacent initiatives contribute 20%; and transformational efforts contribute 70%.

When the company reviewed these findings, it argued initially that it had a 'focused' innovation strategy and an urgent need to reinvent its core products. However, it also recognised the danger of being too focused on the short term. It therefore began a more expansive evaluation of where and how it might innovate. This began a process of participating in accelerators (discussed in the next section) and talking to venture capitalists with a view to setting aside funds to invest in businesses that might deliver those type of innovations.

There is no hard and fast rule about the number of innovations in the portfolio, but the whole must be broad in its scope and have the potential to contribute meaningful value to the parent company. Having all innovations clustered around a particular problem or area of the business is less a sign of focus and more a failure to understand how innovation works. A narrow focus means a gap between the innovation portfolio and the investment thesis concerning how exponential technologies will shape the industry; the appropriate balance (golden ratio) of sustaining and transforming the organisation;

and the company's aspirations for what innovation needs to deliver in terms of incremental sales and/or value.

Establish gaps

Blue Ocean Strategy calls these gaps uncontested market spaces. McKinsey calls them the Green Box. Specifically, it describes a green box as 'the amount of growth that only innovation can produce, after netting out all other possible sources (including market momentum, in-year pricing adjustments, distribution and marketing activities, and M&A).'

From our interviews and experience, we have not come across a company that is this prescriptive about what it needs to achieve. Nevertheless, evaluating a portfolio of innovations only makes sense if it is against something. An investment thesis provides guidance in terms of strategic direction and quantum. If the business has established a view that certain technologies are transforming its industry, then it makes sense to focus its innovation efforts on those same technologies. Equally, it is important to understand whether the business is investing its innovation budget on its business today or the business as it might become.

Financial targets are critical in this assessment because innovations should be contributing to the increase in value of the business. As we said at the beginning of the chapter, innovation is a matter of resource allocation. It is about focusing the company's people, assets, capital, and management attention on the best ideas. It is about the technologies the company will focus on and the 'secret sauce' or unique insights it could expect to bring.

Woodside energy and portfolio structure

Woodside Energy (Woodside) is an Australian petroleum exploration and production company. It is Australia's largest independent dedicated oil and gas company. Woodside defines three types of innovation: continuous improvement (which is the responsibility of the asset/business owner); step change (which involves a dedicated technology team); and disruptive innovation (which dealt with via Woodside Ventures, the new energy division, and FutureLabs). We discuss FutureLabs in more detail in a later chapter, but for the moment, we will simply say that it represents a radical open engagement with partners who are prepared to work on difficult problems with the company. Woodside does not think of itself as managing a single portfolio of innovations, rather it has a series of 'innovation families'. These are clustered around new energy, digital, robotics, oil and gas (where the focus is exploration and development, decommissioning and ways to lower the carbon footprint from new and existing plant). Importantly, they come from within the company's internal R&D and externally from start-ups, universities, and partners.

Fugro and innovation management

Fugro is a multinational engineering company based in Leidschendam, Netherlands with a significant presence in Australia. It provides geotechnical, survey, and geoscience services, and integrated solutions for renewable energy projects from onshore to offshore installations. Fugro has a strong focus on innovation, which is supported by its three centres of innovation worldwide, one of which is located in Australia and includes about eighty staff.

Innovation management for Fugro means following the company's five-step internal 'idea to value' process to develop products and solutions with global application. There is a significant number of potential innovations in the funnel and each year the company selects a subset to work on based on customer demand and their potential (using EBIT as the primary measure). Currently, it is working on over eighty. Each project has timelines, a budget and success measures. Success overall is measured in terms of feedback from the uses: customers, but mainly product managers embedded in the business.

Fugro's innovation teams' focus is on developing technology solutions to accelerate customer sales. Collaborating extensively with third parties, such as universities and other companies, they layer technology solutions onto geotechnical, survey and geoscience services.

Success is about helping the company grow market share. It does this by improving the efficiency and accuracy of its services. An example is the offshore wind turbine foundation design software called GROW, which helps optimise the design and installation of wind turbine foundations. The company is also developing new types of solar panels that are more efficient and easier to install. In the subsea inspection sector, Fugro's key innovation uses autonomous underwater vehicles (AUVs) for surveys. AUVs collect high-resolution data from the seabed, including bathymetry, imagery, and geophysical data, revolutionising subsea inspections by providing more accurate and efficient data collection.

Overall, Fugro's innovation management is about providing its clients with the most advanced and effective solutions for their projects.
The company's strong emphasis on collaboration, both internally and with third parties, has enabled it to develop innovative technologies and solutions that have global applications. The product/solution is handed to product managers who take responsibility for it.

SEEK and portfolio investment

In 2021, SEEK completed a review of its innovation portfolio and announced a new structure. That structure involved the separation of all operating employment marketplace businesses (primarily but not exclusively Asia Pac and Americas (AP&A)) and a newly created SEEK Growth Fund which holds most of its investments in early-stage businesses. AP&A would focus on capturing the significant growth opportunities in its core online employment businesses. The cash flows generated by these businesses would enable ongoing reinvestment to strengthen competitive capability while allowing for payment of dividends. Above all, SEEK announced AP&A would continue to focus on strengthening a culture of customer-focused innovation and commitment to its purpose. The early stage businesses in the SEEK Growth Fund needed substantial additional capital and a willingness to support further sustained periods of larger losses. The company therefore decided that a separate structure was better to make aggressive long-term investment decisions and access external capital. However not all the early-stage businesses went into the Fund and AP&A retained ownership of two large investments (and a handful of smaller ones) which it considered adjacent to the operating businesses.

Managing the portfolio

Managing the portfolio is about maintaining visibility of key information; monitoring milestones and approval/refusal of additional capital investment (or other resources); collaboration with the parent company; governance; accessing performance data quickly to spot and manage risks. There are a range of tools available to facilitate this. However, the companies interviewed tended to take a bespoke approach. For example, a pharmaceutical company told us it was hard to use a single process to manage innovations when responsibilities for innovation were devolved to the business units. Another told us that it had evolved different monitoring for its venture fund which invested in external start-ups, than for innovations developed internally.

Key Questions

We end this chapter with a series of questions for companies to ask themselves to enable them to benchmark their innovation portfolio.

- Does the company have an innovation portfolio?

- How well is it managed and has it grown in value?

- What is its composition (sustaining, adjacent, transformational) and potential (value and business benefit)?

- Is there a gap between the aspirations, investment thesis and portfolio, and what are the appropriate actions to close it?

Chapter 9

Hackathons

Having looked at the innovation portfolio and examined how well it is being managed, we turn to the process of growing innovations. Successful innovators generate twice the sales from new products and services of their less successful peers. Businesses therefore need to develop processes to invest in and scale their innovations to the point where they are big enough to contribute to the business as a whole. However, it is not as simple as setting up an X Prize (which has been running successfully for twenty years) or Google X (which has been running for more than a decade). Instead, companies need to adopt three innovation processes which link together and follow the lifecycle of a start-up. In this chapter, we examine the hackathon.

From acorns to oaks

The oak is often referred to as the king of trees, a symbol of strength and endurance. A fourteenth century proverb, '*mighty oaks from little acorns grow*' speaks of great things that can come from small beginnings. Hackathons take ideas and turn them into minimum viable products. Accelerators take minimum viable products and turn them into start-ups. Corporate venturing take start-ups and invest capital to turn them into scale-ups. Each takes the same ingredients – specific, ambitious goals; societal benefit; breakthrough technology; and competition with outsiders – and applies them to different stages in the company lifecycle. They're what is known in mathematics as fractals like the fern.

Look close, the leaves are shaped like copies of the branches. The whole is built up from the same basic shape repeated at ever smaller scales.

Figure 5, below, illustrates the Moonshot scaling processes from hackathons to corporate venturing. As the innovation scales from idea to scale-up, the investment required and the time spent, increases.

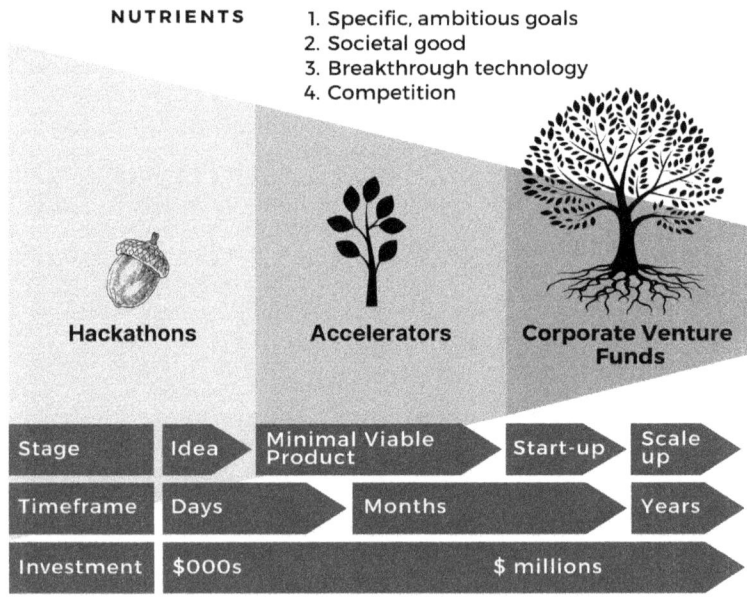

Figure 5. Moonshot scaling processes

We are not suggesting that successful innovators see all their ideas follow this lifecycle in a linear path. What we are saying is that leading innovators are 60% more likely to use these processes than their less successful peers.[20] Moreover, each works on a standalone basis and helps create a dynamic capability to innovate which comes from participating in innovation at different levels. For example, success at the level of a minimum viable product provides evidence to the board and executives of the benefits of increasing scale.

Hackathons, accelerators, and corporate venturing enable companies to innovate in a systematic and managed way. While the funnel gets narrower as the innovations become more mature, the investment required goes in the opposite direction.

What is a hackathon?

A hackathon is an event where participants engage in rapid, collaborative engineering over a short period of time such as twenty-four or forty-eight hours (sometimes sixty-two). The word hackathon is a portmanteau of hacking and marathon, although one would need to be injured, unfit and/or climbing vertically to take forty-eight hours to run 42.195 kilometres, the standard distance for the marathon set by the International Amateur Athletic Federation in 1921.

The original goal of hackathons was to create functioning software by the end of the event, often referred to as a minimum viable product. Hackathons tend to have a specific focus, which can include the programming language used, the operating system, the application, the application programming interface, or, more commonly, a particular type of problem or problem area. Hackathons have evolved and now cover a broader range of goals which include engagement with a target group, creating crowd solutions, and even stimulating creative thinking for the purpose of culture change. Outcomes have also broadened with some programs such as the annual NASA hackathon judging outputs that include PowerPoint presentations, and the Defence Industry hackathons judging stand-alone pitches, or other non-coded solutions.

To maximise the benefit of a hackathon, it is essential to understand why it is being held, what the target outcomes are, how participants will be supported throughout the process, what are the rewards, and the next steps after the event finishes. Readers will not be surprised to discover that the goal often has a benefit to society. Finally, there needs to be an element of competition involving individuals from outside the organisation.

Hackathons run by experienced operators are low investment, rapid feedback, fun ways to engage stakeholders and innovate.

There are many hundreds, maybe even thousands, of hackathons run in Australia every year. Many are internal run by domestic companies.

However, there are a wide range of others from Microsoft's Sentinel Hackathon to GovHack, 'an annual open government data competition held all over Australia and New Zealand'.[21]

How is one run?

Decide the purpose and set expectations

The primary purpose of a hackathon is to stimulate ideas and engage stakeholders. Understanding this and setting the right level of expectations amongst senior executives is therefore important. There are many cases where businesses complain their hackathons did not work because they did not produce implementable solutions. To avoid this misunderstanding, the outcomes must be clearly defined and supported internally from the outset.

Determine the problem statement

A problem statement provides specificity about the area of focus. It is a subset of the specific, ambitious goals that are part of the vision from the earlier chapter. Problem statements must be clear and thoroughly road tested. Examples from hackathons include narrow areas of focus; for example, 'identify safer processes for filter press maintenance', or broader ones, for example, 'Cybercriminals often operate using proxy IP addresses to mask their actual IP addresses for enhanced anonymity. Build a solution that can determine if an IP is actual or a proxy/VPN IP address'. Others that the authors have designed and implemented include how to make a regional town energy self-sufficient within five years, and how to best help young people avoid skin sun damage.

Those examples can easily be linked to societal benefit, in terms of improved safety and/or reducing crime. They are also specific.

Set rewards

From the outset, it is important to determine the prizes and opportunities for the winner(s) to encourage the right level of participation. These can include financial rewards, but the most important prize is furthering the winning idea (that is, a commitment to implementation or deployment, as well as the kudos that comes with being a winner). BHP's hackathons are designed for small business to introduce innovative ideas with the goal of becoming suppliers and is a good example of rewards that are not simply prize money. Rewards will differ depending on the circumstances, but one of the most important metrics to measure the success of a hackathon is that one or several of the ideas gets deployed.

In the programs mentioned earlier, prizes include funding for a three-month project to take the winning idea from concept to minimum viable product. The solutions then gained additional funding for twelve months to take the minimum viable product to full product. One of the other success factors was the commitment of internal resources such as data, trial sites, and expertise, and the inclusion of C-suite executives in the kick-off and judging.

Internal versus external

Many companies can and do run hackathons using just internal resources. Alternatively, it is possible to outsource the management to someone else, or piggyback off an existing hackathon (either one that is industry specific or one that is more generic). In the authors' experience, it is vital the purpose is clear, and the implementation includes diverse voices. Who runs the hackathon is less important to its success than that the event introduces external diversity of participant, mentor, speakers and/or judges. If a company is looking for rapid prototyping or to jump start its product roadmap, it makes sense to introduce new and different voices into the mix. Companies may be sceptical; however, the evidence is overwhelming. To take one example, a recent study demonstrates that diverse teams made better decisions in half the time than less diverse ones.[22]

If the company does not want to have external software developers mixed in with the internal team, then mix different departments together and use external speakers, mentors and/or judges. Xero runs and internal hackathon but brings in outside speakers. Leading biotech company, CSL, hosted a Haemophilia Health Care Hackathon in Tokyo, where medical experts collaborated with CSL's engineers on a brainstorming mission designed to improve the lives of patients with the inherited bleeding disorder, haemophilia. Interestingly, CSL talks about solving a patient's unmet need rather than a customer.

IP ownership

A further point to consider is how the intellectual property (IP) is going to be shared and include that in any waiver that participants need to sign. There is no hard-and-fast rule to this, so it often depends on the type of participants being targeted, as well as the sensitivity of the problem and data being provided. If the hackathon is internal, then any intellectual property will be owned by the company. If the hackathon is external, it is usual for the participants to own the IP they bring to the challenge.

Recruit your cohort

A hackathon can take anywhere from four to eight weeks to organise. Activities include getting facilitators, judges and booking a space. However, the most important activity is recruiting an appropriate cohort. This involves attracting the right balance of technical depth and different skills to ensure creative solutions. It means using a range of communication methods – intranet, direct emails, advertisements, with follow-up phone calls, presentations, and so on. As a final point, dropouts are annoying so do make sure attendees get confirmatory reminders in the run up to the start.

Run the event

It is critical to get to the venue early to confirm everything is ready. This involves chairs, tables, the obligatory beanbags, as well as snacks and food. It is amazing how often the hardware does not work, so do check the Wi-Fi, projectors, power bars and extension cords, audio/PA equipment. It is common practice to have liability waivers and forms for minors. Attendees are welcomed with a formal/informal presentation summarising the objectives, the schedule, and the rules. The welcome should also introduce the organisers, volunteers, speakers, and hackers. Ideally it should also include C-level executives.

Typically, an event will include an opening session on defining the problem statement and team-forming. The next step is for the teams to lay the groundwork on their solution. This is interspersed during the first day with speakers, mentors and breaks to maintain momentum. The second day is about finalising the presentation, presenting it to the rest of the cohort and judges, and announcing the winner(s).

Post-event follow-up

Social media should be used for publicity during the event, and it is also critical to ensure there is sufficient post-event follow-up. This includes generating videos, newsletters, and social media. Combined with this generic communication, is rapid, comprehensive follow-up on the actions that have been agreed. As discussed earlier, the purpose of a hackathon is not just to identify a winning idea. It is about developing a winning culture where innovation can flourish. It is about providing staff with the knowledge and training to improve their ability to innovate and getting commitment from company executives and the board. Everyone that participates must therefore be made to feel part of a team that is contributing.

Do hackathons work?

A recent hackathon documented how participants saw the benefits: 80% said it fostered collaboration; 73% said it promoted an innovative culture; and 71% said it showcased innovative problem solving. Participants love the buzz that comes from collaboration combined with high pressure competitiveness. Leading companies like SEEK and Xero use them. Atlassian is so convinced of the benefits, it has been running them quarterly since 2005.

Of course, hackathons have their detractors. There are few things more demoralising than being told a hackathon is important to the company and then finding none of the executives bother to attend. Moreover, employees can be inspired to work exceptionally long hours on an idea, but due to the competitive nature and compressed timescale, few rise to the top and even fewer make it into implementation.

The entrepreneur and academic, Steve Blank, uses the term Innovation Theater to describe the way some companies run hackathons to appear innovative without working through the harder task of sustaining it. As with any competitive endeavour, the odds are stacked against individual ideas and teams. It is important therefore to be realistic in terms of the expectations of the outcomes and properly resource the follow-up. Some corporations have tried hackathons but determined they did not work because they did not deliver a short-term solution, a clear misunderstanding of the stage of innovation process hackathons solve for, and the outcomes they deliver.

Lessons from interviews and the authors' experience.

- For Atlassian, innovation needs dedicated time and space because 'it's not going to happen on a coffee break'. The company's quarterly hackathon, ShipIt, began in 2005. Business as usual is put on hold so people have the space to create, test, fail and try again. The freedom to work on different areas with whomever the employee wishes, for twenty-four hours (plus a dash of healthy competition) is a massive energy boost. Atlassian credits ShipIt events with numerous product features and internal programs including Jira Service Management, the company's fastest-growing product. SEEK says something similar. Hackathons provide an opportunity for all employees to put tools down for three days and focus on an innovation concept that they believe will drive value both for our organisation and our customers, and for the marketplace in general.

- For SEEK, successful hackathons are about solving a customer problem. SEEK runs them two or three times a year. The company uses them with judging panels to identify the best ideas, which are then piloted and promoted. It begins the process with a question about the customer. Is the proposed solution trying to solve problems for job seekers and hirers? If not, 'it's just novelty'.

- For Xero, hackathons are judged by the CEO, the chief customer officer and chief strategy officer, who ensure feedback is thorough and judging empirical; for example, there are scoring sheets for every idea. Xero makes sure there is proper follow-up. The winners get the greenlight, the losers get full feedback on why their idea wasn't selected. This sends a strong signal about what is important to the organisation.

- Be sure to promote cross-functional collaboration across engineering and non-engineering teams, to facilitate collaboration between different teams, give engineering teams a better perspective on the customer and make the non-engineering teams more vested in the product. As seen earlier, diversity of decision making is critical to better decisions.

- Make time for breaks in between working on the solution. Engaging games and/or food keep the motivation levels up and ensure that a good result is achieved. Experienced users of hackathons tell us that break times should be set up front. The impact is that hackers take these breaks as milestones and are inspired to hack through each of them.

- The danger with a generic problem statement to frame a hackathon is that it does not focus enough on understanding the customer's job to be done, the problem being solved and value proposition. It is important to use the toolset later in the book to ensure these issues are covered.

- Fewer, larger hackathons, on more important issues, are better than running many, but not very well. Over time, there is a tendency amongst some companies to shorten the timescales and reduce the effort in each event to get a better bang for the buck, for example to not involve outsiders in them at all. Hackathons work best when properly organised around all the elements listed in this chapter.

Key questions

- Does the company use hackathons systematically, for a clear purpose?

- How extensive is the effort to ensure suitable program participants?

- Is there a defined process to support solutions developed through the hackathon?

- Have the winning ideas been celebrated, carried forward and outcomes measured?

- Have they met stated objectives?

- Do key executives participate?

- How could they be improved?

- Is there a feedback process to motivate those not selected?

Chapter 10

Accelerators

The next stage of development of an innovation requires market validation, minimum viable product development, building a team, business or internal support, market testing and iteration. Accelerators provide support and resources dedicated to moving an innovation through that process faster that is, accelerating the early stage business or innovation.

What is an accelerator?

If hackathons grow acorns from seedlings, accelerators take them from seedlings to saplings. Start-up accelerators (also known as seed accelerators or incubators) are fixed-term, cohort-based programs that include mentorship and educational components and culminate in a graduation which is usually a public pitch event or demonstration day. Most programs last three to six months, either full or part time. Accelerators can be used to describe programs focused on early-stage start-ups, in contrast to incubators which may take early to late stage start-ups and may last years. For our purposes, the term accelerator is used for both.

Accelerators therefore take ideas a stage further than hackathons to a more formed minimum viable product, a product-solution start-up, or in some cases, through to a scale-up. They are highly effective for independent start-ups, research-commercialisation, and internal corporate innovation projects. To get the best out of them, they need to attract the right type of cohorts, commit funding or access to providers of funding, and provide best practice market experts and potential customers.

Y Combinator, which is usually identified as the first accelerator, was founded in 2005 in Cambridge, Massachusetts. Paul Graham, a computer scientist, formed a three-month boot camp with the idea that investors should be making a greater number of smaller investments, be funding hackers instead of 'suits', and work with younger founders. His collaborator and wife brought expertise from finance and banking to the program. The teams in the first Y combinator accelerator included the founders of Reddit and the man who succeeded Paul as Y Combinator's leader (and now runs OpenAI). Y Combinator has launched companies whose total valuation tops $400 billion. Its alumni include such luminaries as Dropbox, Airbnb, Stripe, CoinBase, OpenAI and DoorDash.

The market for accelerators is well established in Europe, the US, Israel and Australia. Independent accelerators often rent out flexible office space at the same time as running programs. That way the participants can choose to continue to work near the rest of the cohort after they have finished the program. Large companies wanting to get the benefits of accelerators can participate in an existing program or run one themselves. In the latter case, companies must fund and resource them correctly. If a hackathon costs tens of thousands of dollars, an accelerator will cost hundreds of hundreds of thousands. Beyond the dollar investment, companies also need to consider how they will differentiate themselves from existing programs to attract the best start-ups.

The authors conducted desktop research in 2020 that found 162 accelerators in Australia. One they are involved with is the Quantum Technology Exchange (QuantumTX), which focuses on later-stage businesses and corporate innovation. Areas of deep expertise include market testing, growing a solution to address parallel markets, expanding the skillsets of teams, maximising internal resources, and engaging with collaborators. The takeaway being that innovation requires different types of support at different stages of its lifecycle.

How do you run an accelerator?

Goal

Businesses that participate in or run accelerators need to be clear whether they are expecting to use them as an opportunity to invest, a source of ideas to solve internal problems, or a more general marketing and intelligence gathering exercise. Corporate accelerators blend solution development with professional upskilling and strengthening internal collaboration. As with all innovation processes, setting plus internal support are critical to success.

For example, CSIRO uses its ON and PRIME accelerators to move Australian research through the Technology Readiness Levels, and more recently has introduced its 'innovate to grow' accelerators for small to medium enterprises to engage with researchers.

External versus self-run

Australia has professional accelerator service providers so companies have a great deal of options. They can take a low risk, low return option of sponsoring an existing, external program. They can employ external resources to run a program themselves; for example, contract an existing accelerator service provider to deliver a program specifically for their needs, with internal/external or a hybrid of teams participating. Or they can choose to organise and run one internally themselves.

The choices are not mutually exclusive, and may evolve over time from sponsorship, to participation, to dedicated program. Nevertheless, corporate-run accelerators are the minority in Australia, and a number of companies, such as Qantas, have tried them and closed them down. This may be due to a lack of internal ownership, competing internal resources, insufficient internal skillsets, or a change in priorities. Others have grown and are now reaching out globally to expand SME engagement, examples include Aerospace Xelerated, which engages small to medium enterprises with Boeing; M12 which connects enterprise-level Microsoft customers and start-ups; and Lion Unleashed, which helps external incubation with the Lion food and beverage brands.

Several government-sponsored or run industry accelerators have been running for some time; for example, METS Ignited for mining; SheStarts for female founders, and QuantumTX for cross-sector industrial technologies.

Clarifying the offer

Many accelerators offer start-ups money in exchange for a small proportion of the equity, while others offer access to large customers or large markets and are free but can only be accessed via a competitive process.

Y Combinator typically gets 7% of the equity for a $125,000 stake. Sadly, for start-ups in Australia, but happily for those running accelerators, the terms offered here are less generous. Whatever the investment, money can be useful for founders and accelerator alike: the founder can be more focused on the program and not have to worry about feeding themselves; equity investment creates alignment to ensure the company running the accelerator is focused on the start-up's success. Most external, non-corporate accelerators in Australia focus on this model and target traditional early-stage start-ups.

In contrast, government-run and/or sponsored programs are more typically interested in later stage scale-ups. These programs are less likely to request equity, and more likely to focus on jobs and exports (rather than funding) as key measures of success. By not taking equity, they are more suited to later stage businesses who value engagement with corporate customers and market collaboration opportunities.

The key is to clarify the participation offer and make sure that it and the program content is compelling enough to attract the right quality of participant. Companies looking to run accelerators also need to work through and deliver a non-financial benefit to the participants. Every accelerator offers mentoring and coaching, so this is not a differentiator. They all offer introductions to experts, for example, the company's in-house engineering teams. Large businesses start at a disadvantage to independent accelerators because they are perceived as being less likely to attract venture capitalists due to potential conflicts with in-house funding. The non-financial benefit therefore needs to be something that means the start-up is more likely to succeed over the long term. This may include getting it into field trials, introductions to customers and/or suppliers, or investment either directly or in partnership with venture capitalists. Whatever the offer, it needs to be compelling enough to make great start-ups want to apply for and prefer being part of the accelerator over others.

Internal teams

Some corporate accelerators use them to advance internal innovation projects, develop internal talent and capabilities. To maximise this benefit, it is important to ensure that, for the duration of the program, the internal teams are provided with the resources and flexibility to operate as a start-up and not have to rush back to their day job. Another approach is to team internal resources with the external start-ups during the program. This serves to provide knowledge transfer, broaden collaboration opportunities, and ensure participant outcomes are aligned to problems the company wants solved.

Recruitment

Recruiting and selecting appropriate participants requires a focused marketing effort. If the accelerator is run by the company, then it must market its perceived advantages. For example, start-ups in Disney's accelerator are offered access to the company's creativity and expertise, and in return, Disney can help launch innovative products. As the company itself says: 'for nearly a century, Disney has been at the forefront of leveraging technology to build the entertainment experiences of the future. Operating since 2014, the current program is focused on building the future of immersive experiences and specialises in technologies such as augmented reality, non-fungible tokens, and artificial intelligence characters.'[23] Telstra's accelerator, Muru-D, is the largest in Australia. Participants are attracted into the program because of the ability to access Telstra's engineering expertise, product testing facilities, and network of suppliers and customers. A major drawcard is the potential to become a product Telstra channels to its own customers.

Start-ups need to prepare a pitch that is either posted online or made in person. While most applicants are external to the company, successful programs are open to internal applicants as well. The accelerator organisers will require a selection panel to vet and determine the winners which can involve several rounds of judging. Members of an accelerator program are called a cohort. These will include teams from the chosen start-ups because accelerators have learned from long experience never to accept individuals, no matter how brilliant.

Recruitment is not a trivial task and will usually take time, resources and understanding the target participant market. A cohort is typically five to ten companies selected via a competitive process using a selection panel.

Programmed learning

Over three to six months, accelerators provide a tailored program to help participants accelerate the development of their solutions. This includes general corporate services, training on business growth toolsets and capital raising. Later, we highlight a few of these areas such as developing winning ideas, lean management and agile. An important part of the training often involves guided visits to customer facilities. Finally, mentors offer advice tailored to the industry and/or subject matter domains.

Networking

Networking is a critical component, and includes meeting industry experts, subject matter specialists, the cohort, customers and potential funding providers or collaborators. This is why many are run on campuses where the opportunity to meet and mingle is high. Participants report these casual or spontaneous interactions can be as important as the formal program itself. Most large companies should therefore identify a space they can give over to the program. If the accelerator is located away from the company's offices, the organisers need to think how they are going to facilitate networking. For example, 'meet the cohort' functions, visits to important locations such as a network operation centre, or simply arranging for the organising company to locate its own staff next to the start-ups for the duration of the program.

An increasing number of accelerators are being run online, either fully or hybrid. This is particularly the case in a country the size of Australia, with its huge geography with different states and time zones. The benefits include enabling a wider geographic reach for participants and expert speakers, while the downside is the loss of personal interactions and the benefits of in-person engagement.

Demo or showcase day

Programs typically end with some form of showcase event where the cohort gets to present to corporate executives, program stakeholders, potential investors, and other invited parties. Showcases are critical to the start-up, but they also play an important role in promoting the accelerator and its outcomes to internal and external champions. A good idea is to video these events and provide stakeholders with a short summary by way of internal marketing.

The competition at the end of an accelerator program is different from that at the end of a hackathon. Instead of one winner, there is no reason that an entire cohort cannot get funded or see their solution supported through its next stage of growth. Companies therefore need to ensure they have programs in place to stay connected to the cohort after they graduate. The best accelerators have alumni programs to continue engaging participants as they grow and strengthen their offerings.

Accelerators in Australia

It is impractical to provide an overview of all the accelerators in Australia. Instead, this section summarises several to show the alternate models. Many are not operated by a traditional business but by privately owned, specialist innovation service providers. Some corporate accelerators are purely internally focused (for example, Atlassian); others are more traditionally externally focused (for example, BHP, CSL and Telstra); others still are part of the company's social responsibility program (for example, Rio Tinto). The list below is alphabetical.

Atlassian's Point A Solution (an internal, distributed accelerator)

Atlassian's Point A accelerator is a modified version because it is a purely internal program. The company chose this model because it wanted every employee to have the chance of being involved in an innovation program that could scale to meet the company's future needs. Point A was designed to be 'a megaphone for delivering novel solutions to customers'. It has many of the characteristics outlined earlier, but in a distributed manner open to all employees. Google has something similar, known as Area 120, an in-house incubator responsible for products such as Checks, Tables, Stack and ThreadBite.[24] Anyone in the company with a good idea, teams up with interested parties to explore a problem and product that addresses it. They seek out an executive sponsor, who stays with them throughout the process.

They ask themselves:

- Is this aligned with one of the company's strategic priorities?
- Could it be a $100 million business in five to seven years?
- Where does Atlassian play and how can it win?

If the answer to all three is positive, the team moves to the development phase. Here, they receive an initial allocation of three to six members whose roles are backfilled. Teams then spend three months building prototypes with customers to prove their idea is viable. During this time, they meet with their executive sponsor regularly. At the end, they present their solution to a selection panel. If the feedback is positive, the team is expanded and the product is taken to the next stage of commercialisation, typically with a goal of launching in six months. At that point, customers have a chance to be part of Point A by participating in the product's beta program. To date, around 25% of prototypes (equivalent to minimum viable products) have received funding to move to the beta program.

BHP Xplor

BHP Xplor is an external accelerator program dedicated to helping innovative, early-stage mineral exploration start-ups find the critical resources necessary to drive the energy transition. The program is designed with three program tracks: technical readiness, business readiness and operations readiness. The requirements for each program track will be custom fit to meet each participant's needs and the duration of the program may vary (from three to nine months). Xplor offers up to $500,000 in non-dilutive funding to help support the start-up during the program period. On top of this, there are mentors, training, introductions, and in-kind services (tax, accounting etc).

Charge On Innovation Challenge (hybrid accelerator)

The Charge On Innovation Challenge was launched in 2021 by BHP, Rio Tinto and Vale (a Brazilian mining company). It uses many of the components of an accelerator or extended hackathon. There was a competitive process. Vendors and technology innovators were invited from around the world and across industries, to collaborate with the mining industry to present novel electric truck charging solutions. The Charge On Innovation Challenge received interest from over three hundred and fifty companies. Twenty-one were then invited to present a detailed pitch of their solution from which eight were selected. Like the cohort in an accelerator, these solutions were trained in the specific requirements of a group of customers. The eight worked together with BHP, Rio Tinto, and Vale – and sixteen other mining companies – to accelerate commercialisation of interoperable solutions that could safely deliver electricity to large battery-electric off-road haul trucks. Finally, there will be a demonstration or graduation when several of them will be selected for commercialisation.

CSL Incubator

Launched in 2023 and claims to be the 'first and only' accelerator in the country to co-locate its cohort within a major biopharmaceutical company. It is supported by the Walter and Eliza Hall Institute, the University of Melbourne, and the Victorian government.

The Founder Institute

This is one of the most important start-up accelerators worldwide operating in two hundred cities with over five thousand start-ups funded to date. The Founder Institute supports start-ups from various growth phases: from idea to minimum viable product, to early company stage. Its program runs for four months and is mostly operated in after-hours timeslots.

Future Minds Accelerator

This is part of Rio Tinto's $10 million investment program targeted at school-age learners. Developed in collaboration with Amazon Web Services, it aims to prepare young Australians for the digital future, helping fast-track development of skills such as critical thinking, problem solving, automation, systems design, and data analytics. Each start-up is given a $50,000 grant, plus training and mentoring accelerator, and up to $100,000 in AWS credits.

Mining, Equipment, Technology and Services (METS) Ignited

METS is part of the Australian Government's Industry Growth Centres Initiative. Since its inception, METS Ignited has run accelerator programs with funding and support from state and federal governments, local innovation hubs and industry mentors. They have been pitched at scale-up businesses with its SME programs operated by corporate innovation service provider Atomic Sky. Programs have attracted a mix of scale-ups with solutions for the mining and energy resources industries. To date, there have been over twenty programs run for more than one hundred and fifty companies.

Muru-D

Muru-D is the accelerator run by Telstra, Australia's largest telecommunications provider. Six-month programs offer start-ups seed funding, global connections to investors, mentors and alumni, co-working space, masterclasses, and an international trip to a start-up hub.

Orion Energy Accelerator

Orion supports high-impact energy innovations to help New Zealand move towards a carbon-neutral future. The accelerator offers a ten-week program focused on market analysis, market validation, go-to-market strategy, and commercialisation.

There is mentoring from experts in energy, business and start-up growth, networking, and on-site visits.

Skalata Ventures

Skalata Ventures is a start-up accelerator that helps entrepreneurs prepare themselves to scale and expand. It uses a model relying on regional best practices to attain a product–market fit, create a growth engine, and develop a sustainable business model. Start-ups get access to $100,000 to $200,000 of initial funding in exchange for 10% of the equity. At the end of the program, Skalata Ventures may invest up to $1 million in separate rounds over the following twelve months. The firm's Board comprises founders of Australian-born successes Toll and Intrepid Travel, a former university Vice Chancellor, and the founder of Australia's university accelerator program, MAP.

QuantumTX

Since 2016, Quantum Technology Exchange has been accelerating businesses by facilitating collaboration across critical downstream space sector roadmaps from technology innovators in the Mining, Energy, Agriculture and Defence industries. QuantumTX does not take equity stakes in the businesses on its programs.

Do accelerators work?

Telstra's Muru-D has been running for a decade. While it has changed during that time (for example, an office in Singapore has opened and closed), its longevity implies it serves a need for the parent. In a landmark study, four academics examined whether accelerators worked and if so how.[25] They discovered the start-ups that went through an accelerator performed better than similar ventures that did not: they were more likely to raise money, they got more traffic to their websites, they had more employees, and a higher survival rate. Some of the differences might be due to other factors such as that founders in accelerators were able to quit their jobs and work on their ventures full time. However, a statistical analysis of performance indicated that start-up learning in the accelerator was the primary contributor to their success.

The lessons

Three critical program elements drove start-up learning. Mentor and customer interactions were at the beginning of the program, and not during it. While some participants complained this delayed product development, they found common themes emerged from these meetings which were less obvious if they were spaced out over several months. A second determining factor was that successful programs fostered transparency within each cohort via regular check-ins and product demos with peers. Less-successful ones favoured privacy to protect proprietary information. A final success factor was that programs were standardised rather than tailored to each participant's perceived needs. A common schedule forced founders to spend more time considering elements of their business opportunity than they might have if they had been tailored.

At the beginning of the chapter, we defined accelerators as fixed-term, cohort-based programs for start-ups that include mentorship and educational components and culminate in a public pitch event or demo day. However, some organisations chose elements of the accelerator program and tailored them to their unique needs. The key is having a process to take an idea and scale from minimum viable product to start-up and scale-up. As well as those points, the authors note from experience, that access to large customers, experts with sector experience and potential funding networks are key success factors.

Key questions

- Is the company involved in internal and/or accelerators, and if not, why?

- How does it engage with participants, and how do its staff and participants benefit?

- What has been the outcome in terms of working with and or investing in start-ups?

- What is in place to ensure rapid development of solutions beyond the accelerator?

- How could it be improved?

Chapter 11

Corporate venturing

For most large businesses, hackathons and accelerators help to engage stakeholders, progress ideas, and change the culture, but they do not generate significant wealth for the business. The way to do this is by deploying capital in a meaningful way into scalable innovations that solve large challenges. Corporate venturing is the most common vehicle for external innovations.

What is corporate venturing?

Corporate venturing is where a company takes equity stakes in small, high-growth businesses. It complements, but does not replace, traditional R&D, which is more internally focused. Those high-growth businesses may be graduates from an accelerator program or introduced via other avenues. The corporate venturer will most often provide additional resources beyond capital such as management, marketing, sales, and operations. What is important in corporate venturing is the company's commitment to deploying capital (rather than offering services) to grow (primarily third-party) innovations at scale.

Corporate venturing is a subset of venture capital. Venture capital takes a broad cross-section of investors (institutional and high net worth investors), whereas corporate venturing typically comes from only the parent company. Corporate venturing has grown significantly over the past decade. Between 2011 and 2021, annual venture capital investing by corporations grew over fifteen times to $200 billion, according to Pitchbook.[26] This is around 30% of all venture dollars deployed in the US.

Intel Capital is the archetype of corporate venturing. Set up in 1991, Intel Capital's underlying goal to 'earn and learn'; that is, to help its parent, the world's largest semiconductor chip manufacturer, understand technologies and applications that are over the horizon, particularly computing-intensive applications such as artificial intelligence, machine learning, autonomous driving, and fifth-generation, or 5G, wireless.

Most years, Intel Capital invests $300 to $500 million in a combination of new investments and follow-on rounds. The numbers are every bit as mind-boggling as those of Y Combinator. Since it was founded, Intel Capital has invested $12.9 billion in 1,582 companies. Six hundred and ninety-two of those companies have gone public or participated in a merger. While some corporate venture funds prefer to take a supporting role and allow the traditional venture funds to lead, Intel Capital acts more like a conventional venture firm in sourcing deals, leading the majority it invests in, and often takes board seats.

How should corporate venturing be run?

CEO Buy-In

CEO support is one of the most crucial determinants of successful corporate innovation. Even in the best run companies, corporate politics and turf wars can delay or even derail new initiatives. CEO, executive and board support is therefore critical for a high-profile initiative like corporate venturing. This is an investment that will cost tens of millions of dollars and require many years to deliver its full potential. It is impossible to imagine it succeeding without meaningful buy-in from the top.

Involvement of venture capitalists

Given the established venture capital market in Australia and elsewhere, companies can get support from a venture capitalist rather than doing everything themselves. This could be to manage the fund on the company's behalf for example, GrainCorp has done this with Artesian Ventures. Or it could be as a partner, for example, Telstra merged its venture fund with HarbourVest Partners to get greater leverage. Alternatively, the company could run the venturing entirely in house.

Clear objectives

While objectives may change over time, it is important to articulate what a company is trying to achieve at the outset. As we saw with Intel Capital, it could be market intelligence for over the horizon applications which would then feed into a better understanding of the demand for computer chips. In the case of multinational mining and metals company, BHP, it is about the move to clean energy. In other words, while corporate venturing must deliver financial returns, it does not only deliver financial returns.

Differentiation

The venture capital market is mature in Australia. Given this, clear objectives come from a review and thesis about where the market is headed. It also means being clear about how the corporate venturing arm will differentiate itself against other sources of capital. Pure play venture capitalists provide expertise, connections, and independence. Corporate venturers must make a virtue of their lack of independence: that is, demonstrate that links to the parent company will deliver greater value than independence.

One of the ways Intel Capital adds value is via Intel Technology Days (ITDs). The standard ITD brings about ten portfolio companies to one of Intel's customer's premises for a day of introductions, customer briefings, technology presentations and demonstration showcases. Telstra Ventures does something similar, and part of its differentiation is its ability to introduce portfolio companies to its enterprise customers. Telstra Ventures has been able to help its portfolio companies generate more than $640 million in revenue through Telstra's customers.

GrainCorp's venture arm offers portfolio companies links to the group's eleven thousand plus growers, access to an extensive customer network, and a diversified asset portfolio including processing assets to handle a wide range of grains, pulses, and oilseeds. A good example is of how it differentiates itself is its investment in Hone Ag (Hone). GrainCorp Ventures took a minority stake in this start-up that delivers spectroscopy solutions that can be used to evaluate grain (for example, the level of protein or moisture) and soil (for example, carbon). Testing machines are currently costly which limits accessibility, and they only offer a small subset of testing results (for example, grain only). Hone makes and sells handheld devices at a fraction of the cost of traditional machines, meaning growers can test their crops in the field accelerating access to critical data. GrainCorp supports Hone by providing opportunities to engage with growers, trial the technology, and support for its go-to-market efforts.

It requires effort for a company to add value to a start-up investment over and above what a venture capitalist can provide. However, it is critical to success. It may involve customer introductions, access to testing facilities and completing internal trials. However, internal managers may not want their teams losing focus by trialling something that is as yet unproven. Salesmen may not want to introduce start-ups to key customers if they are going to delay or risk a closing a deal.

Engineers are focused on delivering on their day job rather than offering advice to or trialling a start-up's technology, especially when it is not even owned by the company.

Risk appetite

As we have seen earlier, most investments will not return the capital invested in them and only a tiny proportion deliver outsized returns. It is important therefore to articulate the company's risk appetite. What type of start-up is it willing to invest in? What stage in development? How much will it invest? Will it be a lead investor (given that most corporate venturing follows a VC lead)? What proportion of the total investment is it prepared to take? Is the company restricting itself to Australia or prepared to make investments internationally? Are the resources there to ensure a sufficiently large and diverse portfolio to beat the odds? Finally, most, but not all, investments are in equity; however, here is also an increasing market in debt funding scale-up ventures.

According to its website, GrainCorp Ventures 'seeks to invest minority stakes in Seed, Series A or Series B start-ups, aligned to our four investment domains. The scope of investment ranges from $500,000 to $4 million in bold start-ups developing software, hardware and/or new business models that benefit Australian agriculture and food production'. Risk can be offset by working with an established player rather than trying to do everything yourself.

Business plan and budget

The business plan will need to cover the elements listed above as well as the team. Venture capitalists see hundreds of start-up companies for everyone they invest in. They also commonly invest alongside other venture capitalists to share leads and risk. If a corporate venture fund is not outsourcing/partnering with an established venture capital firm, it will need to employ experienced individuals to maximise its chances of success. Alongside the team is the governance structure – investment committee and so on – as well as formal mechanisms to facilitate start-up access to the company's broader resources. The budget needs to include operating costs – the team, support services and due diligence costs – as well as the investing budget or fund size.

The investing budget or fund size will be smaller or larger, depending on the how the company answers the questions in the risk appetite section. Businesses need to be willing to spend tens of millions of dollars on venturing otherwise it is not worthwhile starting. They may choose to do so in a staged manner, but companies need to understand the level of comment over multiple years.

Most companies earmark specific sums in funds to give clarity to management and investors (for example, Atlassian, Gaincorp and IAG). Others do not release the amount to retain flexibility (for example, x15 ventures is funded from CBA's $1 billion annual technology investment envelope.)

A decade-long program

One of the key elements to make a great corporate venturing program is time. Seeing hundreds of potential start-up investments, agreeing valuations, and closing them in a disciplined way, takes time. A $30 million fund at $250,000 per investment means making one hundred and twenty separate investments. This takes years.

Except for Telstra, most Australian corporate venturing is young relative to the American market. The good news is that valuations are lower than in the US (and significantly down on the height of the market); the bad news is that Australia has fewer start-ups to choose from. On top of deploying the fund, it is important to recognise that start-ups take time to mature. Canva, one of Australia's current unicorns, is a decade old. Atlassian was fifteen years old when it listed. For a start-up to reach $100 million in revenue is an amazing achievement, but it may barely register as part of a major multinational. Worse, it might be absorbed and lose the dynamism that that made it so successful in the first place. For all these reasons, companies need to think of corporate venturing as a long-term aspiration.

Corporate venturing in Australia

Australia has a significantly smaller start-up market than the US, both in absolute terms and relative to other measures. In Australia, there are approximately thirty-one venture capital investors with a total of $3.5 billion of funds under management. The average fund size is $113 million. Australian pure-play venture capitalists include Air Tree

Ventures, Square Peg Capital and Blackbird Ventures. The number of Australian businesses with corporate venturing arms is much smaller and more recent. Precise figures are difficult to pin down. However, if 30% of all start-up funding is via corporate venture funds in the US, then the equivalent figure in Australia is between 5% and 10%. This means plenty of opportunities are not getting the funding, especially when we take into consideration that total venture capital funding is already vastly smaller than the US on a like-for-like basis. Below are some examples of Australian corporate venturing.

Atlassian Ventures

Their tagline is 'funding the future of cloud'. In 2022, Atlassian doubled down on corporate venturing, increasing the size of its fund from $50 million to $110 million after its first thirty investments. It invests in two types of business: collaboration apps with the potential to be the next big hit on the Atlassian marketplace; and best of breed apps that are looking to provide value to mutual customers. Investee companies take advantage of services designed to help founders grow their businesses in the Atlassian ecosystem; for example, Fireside Chats, accelerator perks from key partners such as Amazon Web Services and HubSpot, co-marketing, and introductions to key Atlassian subject matter experts.

BHP Ventures

BHP Ventures seek game-changing technologies and emerging companies to help drive sustainable growth. It is focused on making seed investments in early-stage technology companies and start-ups. Since it launched in 2020, it has made fifteen investments as well as built a diverse team spanning the US and Australia.

Coles Nurture Fund

Launched in 2015 by the supermarket parent, it helps small Australian food and grocery producers, farmers, and manufacturers to innovate and grow. This is not traditional corporate venturing. Rather, the $50 million fund offers grants and interest-free loans to fund the development of new market-leading products, technologies, and processes. From Australia's first quinoa processing facility, to fence posts made from recycled plastic, and a state-of-the-art factory to grow grass indoors, the Nurture Fund is unusual in that it is an environment, social, and governance (ESG) measure, rather than an innovation and wealth-creating initiative.

Commbank's x15 ventures

Launched in 2020, x15ventures is funded from CBA's $1 billion annual technology investment envelope with its own delivery model and dedicated management team. It works with Microsoft and KPMG to deliver expertise and support for digital innovators. x15 Ventures targets digital solutions within financial services and adjacent industries seeking pre-seed to pre-series B funding.

Graincorp Ventures

Graincorp was launched in 2021 with a $30 million fund. Investments range from $500,000 to $4 million in start-ups developing software, hardware and/or new business models that benefit Australian agriculture and food production. Its focus is on analytics and optimisation, smart supply chains, biotechnology and sustainability and the circular economy.

IAG – Firemark Ventures (Firemark)

IAG is focused on advanced technologies which are important to the future of Australia's largest general insurer. This includes machine learning, computer vision, deep analytics and IoT. Firemark has made thirty-three investments across eighteen portfolio companies and embedded new technologies in the parent company following successful internal trials. Firemark Ventures launched its second $75 million fund in March 2022. It is part of IAG's separately structured Innovation and Venturing Hub.

NAB Ventures

NAB Ventures focuses on four areas of financial services: technologies that help small and medium business customers manage all of their financial needs (including banking, tax, invoicing, and payroll) at every stage of their journey; innovations that support retail customers through the full home ownership journey; ones that build easier, faster, richer payments for customers; and finally, ones that help customers build, monitor and manage wealth. It has made thirty-three investments and six exits (via a sale or floatation).

SEEK Growth Fund

In 2021, SEEK split its investments into a separate fund with its own management. This involved SEEK transferring assets to the new fund valued at $1.2 billion, comprising its holdings in Online Education Services and a number of other early-stage ventures.

Telstra Ventures

Telstra Ventures is more than a decade old, and has offices in Syndey, Shanghai, and California. Since 2011, it has made eighty-eight investments that have resulted in thirty-three liquidity events (either M&A or IPO), with seventeen of those achieving unicorn status and five achieving decacorns status (a valuation above $US10 billion).

Telstra Ventures and Whispir

This Australian business provides a good example of how good corporate venturing works over many years to provide funding, sales opportunities, introductions, and other benefits. In 2001, Whispir was founded as a conversation platform for business-critical communications. Companies plug existing channels and business systems into the platform, and it helps manage internal and external communications.

In 2012, Telstra Ventures invested and built a channel relationship with Whispir. Telstra accelerated its growth by selling it to its customers and using it internally. Several years later, Whispir raised further funding with Telstra Ventures and others. Telstra then assisted Whispir's entry into Indonesia via a joint venture with Telkom Indonesia. In 2019, the company floated on the Australian Stock Exchange (ASX) raising $47 million, with a staff of one hundred and forty across Australia, New Zealand, Singapore, Indonesia, and the US. Telstra remains a key partner.

Does corporate venturing work?

The answer depends on the goal, stage and focus of growth, plus how innovation is being applied both inside and externally to the company. Corporate venturing may be seen as a way for organizations to learn faster; to outsource research and development; to get leverage on the future strategy of investments; to create options for future acquisitions; or to encourage the ecosystem. Intel would not have been involved in corporate venturing for thirty years if it did not work for them. However, while there are certainly highly successful corporate venturing programs, it is not possible to conclude about corporate venturing as a whole.

This is in part because the question of success itself begs the question of against what. In-house research and development is risky. A well-run corporate venturing fund can help a company respond to changes in markets and gain a better view of threats. It can stimulate demand for a company's own products and the returns may be attractive. However, some corporate leaders we interviewed had a different view on venturing. They saw it as a distraction from internal innovation and core business growth. Being separate meant it was hard to apply the innovations to the core. Being owned meant that it might even put off some customers.

Work by Ernst and Young suggests the most active corporate venturing firms outperform their peers and the overall market in both short term and the long term performance.[27] However, it is difficult to unpick the contribution of corporate venturing in this figure as businesses do not normally publish the returns from their funds. Other research in the US and Europe suggests they do create value for the investor in aggregate and the success rates is similar to, or slightly lower than, the success rates of venture capital funds.[28] Finally, studies have also shown that during their first three years as public companies, firms backed by corporate venturers have better stock price performance than companies backed by traditional venture capital.

What is clear is that corporate venturing is popular amongst large corporations in the US and Europe. Some of Australia's leading companies have launched venture funds in the past decade but as a whole the corporate venturing market is much smaller as a percentage of domestic venture capital investments. There have been successes. However, it would be wrong to suggest that most corporate venturing programs succeed. Their average life cycle in the US has been estimated at about four years, implying many are closed down well before they had chance to deliver.

Changing attitudes

A recent article in *Global Corporate Venturing*[29] points out that for the first time after four economic cycles, corporate venturing has proved more resilient than venture capital, having seen much less of a market pullback in 2022 than the venture capital sector overall. There are reasons to believe corporate venturing may well become more relevant for investors in the future. First, the increasing importance of ESG investing has blurred the boundaries between environmental and long term investment. Second, there is a renewed recognition that small companies can be central to large company growth. Finally, public equity markets have underperformed private equity and venture capital over the long term and investors are therefore interested in new ways to support their public investments.

What are the lessons?

Unlike hackathons and accelerators, corporate venturing requires a large investment over a significant time. Lessons for Australian companies looking to create follow.

Take first steps with venture capitalists

The venture capital ecosystem is well established, so it makes sense to work with experts in the area to determine the goals and structure of a potential separate corporate venturing unit. This can be achieved in a variety of ways: investing as a limited partner in one of their funds; forming a joint fund; co-investing in specific businesses; and presenting internally generated solutions for third-party investment. These can form the basis of a corporate venturing fund in the future, or the company can continue investing in a more ad hoc manner.

Many of the most successful corporate innovators create internal funds but most also invest strategically in well-run, early-stage funds to access start-ups, university research and a route to radical innovation. By way of example, Skalata Ventures is a great example of how corporations can leverage established systems and know-how. According to Rohan Workman, Co-Founder of Skalata Ventures: *While venture capital funds can deliver well-diversified exposure to innovation (and direct profit returns), the true value for corporations is access to disruptive start-ups and founders with diverse thinking and expertise.*

Skalata Ventures was founded on the basis of bringing the worlds of academia, business and venture capital together - something that hadn't previously been done in Australia.

Experience matters

This is one area in which companies should leverage existing expertise as the pitfalls, like the benefits, can be meaningful. According to INSEAD research, hiring at least one experienced venture capitalist correlates with ongoing success.[30]

Alignment matters

Research shows that while it is often hard to link growth of shareholder wealth to corporate venturing, there is evidence that investors are concerned if the company's investments are not perceived to be aligned with the core business. Diversification is not a reason for corporate venturing.

Get the processes and success measures right

Innovation moves at pace, so it is important to define the right structures and processes to enable fast decision making, fail quick and impact outcomes. Related to this is the advantage of creating an internal 'fund' of committed capital to be invested over a set period of time.

A downturn is an opportunity

It is interesting that Atlassian has doubled its corporate venturing fund as the market has declined because companies that have come out best from previous downturns have been those that maintained or increased their investment in start-ups in a disciplined way.

Corporate venturing or corporate venturing

The corporate challenge with innovation is finding an appropriate approach to deploy meaningful amounts of capital into scalable innovations that drive real value. A parallel challenge is how to innovate with impact while not distracting focus from core business. A corporate venturing arm is a formal, proven way to do this. It is a way to spot external opportunities alongside the more traditionally internally focused R&D.

External opportunities may be partners to enhance core sales (for example, Telstra); a way of discovering more about market trends and growing use of a platform (for example, Atlassian); or a way to enhance R&D as part of strategic shift (for example, BHP). They require careful management. Nor is corporate venturing right for every stage in the company's life cycle. For example, Xero has grown threefold over the past few years and decided the time is not right for corporate venturing because there is so much growth in its core offering. But it is worthwhile repeating the observation that Australian companies use corporate venturing far less than their international counterparts. They also partner less with third parties on R&D. Both factors suggest, it is important to consider the appropriateness as part of an innovation strategy.

To conclude, companies need to develop a flexible funding mechanism to ensure internal and external ideas get the capital they need to realise their full potential. Corporate venturing is a proven way to do this for externally developed start-ups; however, companies might develop their own internal corporate venturing process that is better suited to their needs. The elements include spotting and turning ideas into minimum viable products, scaling them to become start-ups, and scaling them again. By consistently investing time and effort, leading companies create a virtuous cycle that leads to sustained success.

In his book *Good to Great* (2000), business consultant Jim Collins introduced the concept of the flywheel which has become a widely used metaphor for how businesses build momentum. The flywheel represents a continuous cycle of effort and investment that generates results and creates positive outcomes, leading to even greater success. Collins emphasises the key to the flywheel is consistency – sustained effort and investment over time builds momentum and creates a self-reinforcing cycle. At first, it requires a lot of effort to get the flywheel moving, but with each turn, it becomes easier, and momentum builds. This can then be harnessed to generate more energy and drive the flywheel even faster.

Key questions

- How effectively does the company fund the growth of its portfolio of innovations?

- How does it tap into external markets trends and early disruptors?

- Does the company have a clear idea of how it could successfully launch and sustain a corporate venturing initiative?

- How could it improve?

Chapter 12

WINNING IDEAS

Underpinning innovation practices used by leading companies are a set of tools. These include the ability to develop and select winning ideas whether they are internal or external. The use of methodologies to plan implementation, such as the Business Model Canvas, Crowd Innovation, Lean Management and Agile. Getting the right people and culture. Finally, collaboration around research, notably with government. Leading innovators are far more likely to use these tools and collaborate externally than their less successful peers. This chapter focuses on winning ideas.

Winning ideas consist of the problem to be solved, the unique solution, a great team, traction in the market, and a sensible valuation. Recognising and being able to evaluate each of these elements is a core skill for any company, strategic leader, or intrapreneur.

Figure 6 Our innovation process

Problem to be solved

The single biggest criterion for applied innovation is clarity about the problem to be solved; or more specifically, a clearly formed and tested hypothesis about a problem in an area that is big, known, and where the start-up or innovator can develop a unique solution. We learned earlier that venture capitalists earn their returns from a small number of investments that deliver outsized returns. It follows that any corporate innovator must focus on major challenges that can deliver significant upside. Unsurprisingly, the first part of Google X's three-part innovation formula is that the innovation must address a huge problem. And one of the group's key ways of working on these problems is to fall in love with it and not the solution.

However, inexperienced founders can get carried away by the massive size of a market without really understanding its dynamics or the problem they are working to solve. We commonly use the saying: 'Is there a gap-in-the-market AND a market-in-the-gap?' By contrast, when established businesses try defining these problems, they will often start with a series of constraints about the markets in which they operate and the capabilities of their own firm. This is very different from a Blue Ocean thinking of looking towards users to find new markets and uncontested spaces.

TAMs (total addressable market), SAMs (served available markets) and target markets are obligatory parts of any growth strategy and a source of much derision from those reviewing them. We recently spent time with a business that combined satellite imagery from different sources to help accelerate engineering infrastructure decisions. However, there is already an Australian business in this space owned by a US private equity firm. Any start-up satellite imagery company therefore needs to understand the value chain and the competitive dynamics of the market to present not just the TAM, but the realistic target market.

The authors prefer the term 'problem to be solved', because it focuses on a customer's unmet need, which leads naturally onto the unique solution (covered in the next section). So, the 'problem to be solved' needs to be large, but genuinely addressable. It also needs to focus on unmet needs.

A good example is Foxtel which, as mentioned earlier in the book, has suffered with the development on over-the-top streaming services. Whilst Presto did not resonate with viewers, it has continued to innovate (with streaming offerings Binge and Kayo) and has spotted an opportunity in the very proliferation of on-line streaming services for an aggregation platform.[31] Anyone who has tried unsuccessfully to find a show they want to watch on a multitude of different streaming services knows that the sheer choice on offer has become a problem for consumers who want to watch what they want to watch irrespective of the service.

Unique solution

Innovators often compete against incumbents with deeper pockets, access to capital, existing customers, and more experience. To succeed, they need to surround themselves with an excellent team, be in a large/growing market, and create a solution that is – if not unique – hard to replicate.

Canva is an Australian unicorn that has received broad public exposure in recent years. The business was founded by Melanie Perkins. While teaching fellow students basic computer design as part of her communications and commerce studies, Melanie identified a challenge. The process of designing content using available software was expensive and required extensive training. Yet many potential users would benefit from tools and templates for simpler tasks such as parents printing school posters, yearbooks, or flyers.

Her insight was that instead of creating the designs in Adobe Photoshop or Microsoft, converting, and saving them, then arranging printing, it would be much simpler if there was a set of free tools, templates, and basic macros accessible to all.

These could cut out the middle-man design consultants and open a massive untapped market for consumers. At first blush, it seems unlikely that a small Australian start-up could complete with global enterprises like Adobe and Microsoft. However, both organisations are in the business of subscription-based professional publishing, so the 'amateur' market was largely untapped. Taking advantage of online access to expand globally, Canva has now grown to over seventy five million users and five million subscribers.

> People don't want to buy a quarter-inch drill. They want a quarter-inch hole!
>
> Theodore Levitt

Clayton Christensen put it elegantly in the Innovator's Solution when he said: 'competitiveness is far more about doing what customers value than doing what you think you're good at. And staying competitive as the basis of competition shifts necessarily requires a willingness and ability to learn new things...' Christensen describes understanding customer needs as the 'jobs to be done'. For instance, most people would say they buy a car to get from A to B. However, automotive companies know customers do not buy a Mercedes-Benz to get from A to B. They buy it to feel good, to achieve status amongst their friends, or demonstrate they have a certain position in their lives. Utility (getting from A to B) is subordinate to a deeper need (status and reward).

Similarly, it is superficial to say that Canva provides publishing solutions. What Canva's clients want is not publishing software, but beautiful designs delivered simply and cost effectively. This is the power of the jobs to be done. It helps us understand the outcomes customers are truly after because they do not buy products and services, they buy or hire solutions.

Amazon Web Services (AWS) and Atlassian case studies

At first sight, moving from online shopping to enterprise-grade technology sounds risky. However, when Amazon began scaling its own IT architecture, it realised it had created solutions that could be used by its customers as well. AWS was born in the early 2000s. Developing solutions to improve the speed of software engineering, allowed teams to focus on innovation instead of IT problems. The success of AWS was unexpected, hundreds of applications were built on the platform in the early years. By 2021, it reported 32% yearly growth and had more than a 30% share of the $42 billion cloud market.

Atlassian is an Australian unicorn. Initially funded by Mike Cannon-Brookes and Scott Farquhar with a $10,000 credit card debt, its name derives from Greek mythology, an ad hoc derivation from the titan Atlas who was punished by being forced to hold up the Heavens. Atlassian started as a support company for customer service teams, but with the success of its bug-tracking software, it pivoted to being a software business. Last year, Atlassian's sales were close to $3 billion.

There are several similarities between these two case studies. Both companies started with problems they knew and understood extremely well. A way to vastly improve the odds of success is to start with a major challenge that you know, either internally because you have worked on it, or externally because your customers are struggling with it.

A second tip is to focus on future demand, rather than the existing market. In the case of Amazon, the company sought to improve the speed of its own software development. However, it soon realised its customers would face the same constraints as they scaled. In the case of Atlassian, it was the insight that helping companies' customer support teams, as it had done itself internally in an ad hoc way, was not scalable and there needed to be software tracking in place to measure, monitor and eliminate bugs.

Finally to maximise impact, the solution needs to be hard to replicate. In the case of Canva, a deep understanding of the market shows that there are vast numbers of individuals who want to produce beautiful designs simply and not need to be trained in complex software programs or incur long-term licensing costs. Following Clayton Christensen's approach, Canva focused on a proportion of the market that was not well served by the incumbents because it was not perceived to be attractive.

At this point, it is worthwhile thinking about the technology in the unique solution. The MAYA principle stands for 'most advanced yet acceptable' technology, and is a framework developed by Raymond

Loewy (often referred to as the father of industrial design). There is a delicate balance between developing a unique solution for an imagined future and what can be commercialised today. As we discovered in Part 1 of the book, effective innovations often take existing ideas or technologies and apply them in novel ways. Canva introduced a freemium model to design enabling millions of users get free access to beautiful designs and templates. It did not need cutting-edge technology to be successful. If you look at the evolution of Apple's iPod, you find it gradually loses its extra buttons and gains a more streamlined interface as users become more accustomed to its features. In other words, rather than starting off with something that is too strange, the technology evolves as customers become more knowledgeable. A useful metric to test the winning idea's chances of success is whether at least 40% of surveyed customers indicate that they would be 'very disappointed' if they no longer have access to a particular product or service.

In the chapter on accelerators, we mentioned research that shows the most effective time to have training is at the beginning of the program. The reason is that it allows founders to refine and clarify their winning idea, notably the problem to be solved and the unique solution. There is significant overlap between problem/solution and product/market fit.

Team

> Put 80% of your effort into building a quality team. Give me a great team in a terrible market any day over a great market and a terrible team. It's about the power of a collective team to execute and move according to market changes. I can't overstate that.
>
> Matt Rockman, Co-founder of SEEK

It is no surprise that one of the key things corporate leaders and venture capitalists come back to again and again is the team. While entire libraries have been written about brilliant founders, the reality is that the successful application of innovation relies on teams. The logic with considering the team as a core component of a winning idea is to back the jockey not the horse. Any innovation project will change as it evolves, even more so as the project becomes embedded in the organisation's DNA: maybe it has the wrong product/market fit, the wrong plan or business model. If the innovation is good, a good team will execute it well; if it is poor, a good team will make the required pivot – both are strategically strong outcomes.

So, what makes a successful, high-impact innovation team? A common answer is that prior experience, product knowledge, and industry skills. While these are certainly important, and indeed investors will take comfort in them, they are not sufficient to succeed. A research study found that while experience broadens the resource pool and helps people identify opportunities, successful teams need soft skills to thrive. Specifically, a shared entrepreneurial passion and strategic vision are key to superior performance. This ties back to starting with a Moonshot then developing teams based around entrepreneurial appetite and suitable emotional intelligence.

The final element of a winning team is diversity of experience, background, and outlook. Atlassian's formula for successful innovation is: **freedom + focus + curiosity + cognitive diversity.**

Founders spend a great deal of recruiting. So, it is worthwhile examining some of the red flags and how to overcome them.

The big dog who only manages

One of the biggest red flags is the senior manager who has successfully worked for a large organisation. The benefit of this individual is immediate credibility with division leaders and other support networks. The challenge is that the structure which facilitated the big dog's corporate role and career does not necessarily align to the hectic day-to-day of Moonshot application. Often, they are too used to having mountains of data, meetings arranged by a secretary or travel coordinator, and a team working with processes and procedures that have been developed for established systems. The key is to understand what they have been doing day-to-day in their prior job, their flexibility and whether they have the appetite for the type of unstructured work that accompanies the early stages of an external-facing innovation project.

The prima donna coder

The technical domain expert who believes they can solve anything because they have done well historically and believe they are head and shoulders above their peers. Very often, this individual will have exceptional technical skills that have been recognised in a prior job. This sort of individual will do well in case study-based interview questions, so the trick is to try behavioural ones to determine their underlying personality traits. An example might be: give me an instance of when you helped a colleague solve a problem or when you influenced someone to help you when they did not work for you. The selection process for the innovation team should focus on specific, real examples, rather than theoretical case studies, and get the individual to describe what they learned and how they engaged with different types of stakeholders.

The sell-anything salesman

Salespeople need to be confident to do their job. However, the challenge with innovation projects is that by their nature, they evolve in an iterative basis. The company identifies a problem, forms a hypothesis, develops a minimum viable solution, tests with a target market, gathers feedback then iterates. The product is therefore not perfect, which leads to a precarious and evolving relationship with customers, be they internal or external. Star salespeople will often come from sales-driven companies with mature products. The risk is that they oversell, causing disappointment and frustration with those customers who are needed to provide feedback, support, and traction. Behavioural questions are important here as well, but the focus should be to get the individual to discuss how they set expectations with the customer and examine situations where the customer was not happy with the product and how they dealt with it.

Traction

Traction is the primary milestone marker of progress and the baseline for future investment. It shows stakeholders the innovation is solving the problem for its target market in a way that people are prepared to pay for. For market-facing products, it demonstrates demand, pricing models and the potential for scale. It provides proof of product–market fit along with validation of the roadmap, and evidence that the team is delivering progress against plan – all of which minimises stakeholder risk.

Traction builds the ground for the 'ask'. It reduces the risk of not receiving executive support by providing data on which budgeting models can be more reliable, shows where the intended users are engaging and how they are using, providing the framework for the next phase of work. Evidence of traction can be soft or hard depending on whether it is quantified or not, and the extent to which the company has access to financial or non-financial metrics.

Table 2, below, represents the different type of measures that could be used to demonstrate traction.

SOFT	Non-quantified metrics such as awards won, testimonials and customer feedback.
HARD	Quantified metrics such as net promoter score, patents or licences granted, Government grant awarded, number of staff recruited, and retained.
NON-FINANCIAL	More important for minimum viable product and/or beta testing stage, such as the number of users/downloads, users and percentage of active users, user ratings/ feedback, time on site, pages visited, returning visitors and time saved/ gained by users.
FINANCIAL	More important for scale-up stage, such as a percentage of share of wallet, sales / monthly recurring revenue, revenue, margin and profit growth, cost/revenue per unit, subscriptions and churn rates, customer acquisition cost, cash flow/ cash burn.

Table 2. Financial and Non-Financial Metrics

Reasonable valuation

The end of any innovation pitch will involve an ask: what resources the corporate innovation team or start-up business requires, how the funds will be used, burn rates and key performance indicators, plus some idea of valuation.

Just like start-up investors, internal stakeholders and project champions receive different returns for different stages of investment. Seed support requires a higher level of championing within the organisation, usually from the CEO, and ideally at board level, depending on the size of the business. The investment thesis helps provides the framework in which the innovation team can operate effectively. There is likely less data available and no traction at this point, so innovation rarely succeeds without that Moonshot level support.

The first round after the seed stage is called Series A. This will take the start-up from idea to developing business model. In the corporate world, it is the stage where the strategy is in place, and the team has gained enough traction to pitch for more permanent budget and staffing allocation.

By Series B, a start-up should have a decent user base and have proven that it is on the path to success on a larger scale. Series B funding is used to grow the company so that it can meet these levels of demand. In the corporate environment, it is the stage at which the lead intrapreneur pitches to take steps such as split off the team into a separate business unit, commit more formally with external collaborators, and/or explore a corporate venture fund.

Replacement cost

Traditional businesses are valued via three methods. *Replacement cost* looks at the cost of replicating what the start-up has developed (for example, a software solution) and uses this as a benchmark for what it might be worth. The advantage of this method is that it is easy to track and demonstrate. The downside is that cost estimates are often low because they underestimate both the risks involved to get to this stage and the value of any revenue streams.

Comparable multiples

The second method is *comparable multiples*, which involves looking at the valuation of similar transactions in the market (mergers, acquisitions, or capital raisings) or similar listed companies. Multiples can be financial (for example, eight times profits) or non-financial (for example, $1,000 per subscriber). The advantage of this method is that it provides a level of objectivity to subjective valuations. The disadvantage is that businesses, particularly start-ups, are rarely comparable.

Discounted cash flow

Finally, *discounted cash flow (or net present value)* provides a measure of the company's intrinsic value based on its business plans and projected cash flow discounted by its weighted average cost of capital. Theoretically, this is the best method to use because it reflects the unique circumstances of the business. In practice, however, the disadvantage is that it relies on perspectives of future prospects which are uncertain and subjective.

Getting to a sensible valuation is hard for a start-up business with limited to no financial track record. In many cases, it can be even harder for a corporate innovation project. In the corporate environment, there are competing needs for the existing core business, pulls from multiple directions on staff time, and potential brand impacts to consider.

The best advice is to support the valuation of the project with as much information as possible about its potential impact, both direct financial impact plus flow-on benefits to the company.

Try multiple valuation methods and triangulate them.
Include information on how it will open other opportunities, develop staff capabilities, support company culture, and apply the Moonshot goals of the organisation.

If possible, obtain valuations from similar businesses or business innovation initiatives and add in how start-ups in the applied area were bought and sold as another benchmark.

Stage development method

The *stage development method* or the *development stage valuation approach* is used by angel investors and venture capital firms to come up with a quick valuation range for a start-up. This method uses the various stages of funding to decide how much risk is still present. The further the business is along the stages of funding the less the present risk. A typical Series A in Australia might be valued at $5–10 million.

An investor might build that up something like the following table.

STAGE DEVELOPMENT METHOD

STAGE	COMMENTARY	VALUATION
Problem to be solved	Insightful understanding of large market opportunity	$1-2m
Unique solution	Final product or technology prototype	$1-2m
Team	Strong team with proven capability	$1-2m
Traction	Strategic alliances or partners, or signs of a customer base	$1-2m
Traction	Paying clients	$1-2m

Table 3. Stage Development Valuation

There are significant subjective assumptions with this approach. Nevertheless, what it does do is quantify those assumptions, allow some type of benchmarking, and link progress of the start-up to changes in its valuation.

Fair market value is the price a product, asset, or company, would sell for on the open market assuming both buyer and seller are reasonably knowledgeable, behaving in their own best interests, free of undue pressure, and given a reasonable period to complete the transaction. This section is called 'reasonable valuation' because some businesses approach funding with unrealistic expectations. As the definition above outlines, value is what someone is prepared to pay. This is similar with sourcing corporate innovation budgets in what someone is prepared to champion and put their name/ career trajectory behind. Do not be greedy. It is better to get the funding, so the project gets to the next stage, than to spend six months not getting it at all.

Rinse and repeat

While the odds of creating a hugely successful innovation are small, getting better at creating and identifying winning ideas is a process that can be learned. Iteration – apply, rinse, repeat – and feedback are critical.

There is a famous quote by Steve Jobs. "Some people say give the customers what they want, but that's not my approach. Our job is to figure out what they're going to want before they do. Henry Ford once said, 'If I had asked people what they wanted, they would have said faster horses'. People don't know what they want until you show it to them. That's why I never rely on market research. Our task is to read things that are not yet on the page."

A key aspect of innovation is that it is difficult to define, let alone quantify, an unmet need for something that by definition does not yet exist. Most users thought the mobile phone was for talking rather than a pocket-sized computer. Having noted that, and with due deference to Steve Jobs, the vast bulk of successful innovations come from deep insights into customer behaviour and their frustrations, as well as iterations of potential solutions. It is wise to include their feedback because the 40% rule mentioned earlier is a very powerful tool. It is wiser to repeat the process.

Persistence improves the idea and the chances success. Canva was rejected by over one hundred venture capitalists before it successfully raised money. However, it matured and developed as it took in these rejections. In its search for funding, the company founders unsuccessfully ambushed a dinner hosted a Silicon Valley venture capitalist and went kitesurfing in Maui trying to meet investors. Finally, persistence paid off.

Winning ideas consist of the problem to be solved, the unique solution, a great team, traction in the market and a reasonable valuation. Recognising and being able to evaluate each of these is a core skill for any business looking to innovate. This applies to start-up teams, managers running the teams, credit committees and executives making decisions about innovation.

Key questions

- Does the company have an approach to recognising and evaluating winning innovation ideas?

- What are the lessons in terms of how successful this has been?

- How deeply ingrained are these lessons in the company's culture?

- How aligned are the winning idea with the overarching company strategy and investment thesis?

Chapter 13

Implementation planning

The previous chapter looks at winning ideas as a driver of innovation. In this chapter, we examine how to plan implementation. The Business Model Canvas is a common tool to put the core elements of a start-up onto a single page. Crowd innovation is a way to engage with external stakeholders to attract a broader range of diverse thinking. Lean Management and Agile are a set of tools and roles that help teams structure and manage their work. Finally, there are a range of tools to facilitate communication with a distributed workforce.

Business model canvas

A business model is nothing more nor less than a representation of how a business makes (or intends to make) money. The nine building blocks that have come to be called the Business Model Canvas were initially proposed by a Swiss PhD, Alexander Osterwalder. It has become a common tool to put the core elements of a start-up onto a single page.

The nine building blocks consist of the following. The *value proposition* of what is offered to the market and consists of an explanation of the type of customer problem that is being solved. A value proposition addresses specific *target customer segments* via communication and *distribution channels* to form *customer relationships*. These relationships will be very different if the product or service is self-serviced or co-created with the customer. *Key resources* are the capacities needed to make the business model possible, which may be physical, financial, or technical. These resources must be configured into *key activities* to implement the business model. Activities might include production for hardware or problem solving for a services business. Beyond that will be *key partners* who make a business model happen generally, but not always, suppliers. Finally, there are the *revenue streams* generated by the business model and the *cost structure*.

Yes, but in practice...

Developing a business plan can be a lengthy and arduous exercise. Business Model Canvas is a visual template for identifying and organising different elements of a business model. Its great advantage over traditional business planning is that it can be developed by a team jointly in less than an hour. This means teams can get a common understanding of the overall business model they are working towards agreement about where there are gaps in their understanding, and a joint focus on what needs to be achieved next.

In most cases, corporate innovators will be required to develop and deliver a business plan. The Business Model Canvas can therefore be an extremely valuable tool in that process. Fundamentally, a plan on a page forces the innovator or start-up leader to understand the essential factors and levers. It provides a framework for the key points of the more detailed business plan, serves as a summary document, and can help feed the slide topic headers for the often-required power point presentation.

Crowd innovation

A range of tools are available to tap into crowdsourcing to generate fresh and innovative ideas, solutions, and designs. Crowd innovation leverages the collective intelligence and creativity of a diverse community by using open social extensions.

Crowd innovation, also known as open innovation, is a process by which companies invite external individuals or groups to contribute to their innovation process. Here are some recent examples of large corporations using crowd innovation:

- Lego Ideas: Lego's crowd innovation platform allows anyone to submit their own ideas for new Lego sets. If an idea gets enough support, Lego will consider turning it into a product. For example, the platform resulted in the creation of a set based on the TV show *Friends*.

- Coca-Cola Freestyle: Coca-Cola's Freestyle machine allows customers to mix and match their own soda flavours. Coca-Cola used crowd innovation to develop the machine, working with external partners to design the user interface and optimise the technology.

- Rio Tinto's Pioneer Portal is looking for original ideas that could transform the mining industry. The Pioneer Portal is a platform to identify and select innovative solutions. It is open to start-up entrepreneurs or existing businesses, with small-scale ideas or proven solutions and technology.

- Samsung has a long history of open innovation with its Innovation Challenge program. This program invites start-ups and innovators from around the world to pitch ideas with the goal of collaborating on new products and technologies.

- Unilever's Foundry platform allows start-ups to collaborate with Unilever to develop new products and services. The company partnered with a start-up to develop a smart packaging solution that uses LED lights to indicate the freshness of food products.

Compared to traditional closed innovation where ideas are generated within the company or industry, crowd innovation opens up idea generation to a larger, more diverse group. This may include customers and the general public. It has become increasingly popular among global brands seeking to uncover valuable ideas and innovate outside traditional R&D departments.

Crowd innovation is also a way to achieve diversity and inclusion in innovation. To maximise the benefits of crowdsourcing, businesses must define problems in a way that enables participants to tackle complex and comprehensive issues. Additionally, they must structure a campaign to facilitate the cross-fertilisation of ideas and encourage participants to share their best ideas instead of withholding them.

While there are risks with crowdsourcing, such as rogue participants seeking to undermine the project or internal cultural biases that may stifle radical ideas, crowd innovation remains a powerful tool for generating fresh and innovative ideas.

Leading innovators are far more likely to use it than their less successful peers. Implementing it offers numerous potential benefits such as increased employee engagement, improved customer satisfaction and a competitive advantage in the marketplace. Steps to ensure its success start with selecting a suitable crowd platform to provide the process tools. The steps to run a crowd innovation program are below:

- Launch a campaign targeting a strategic opportunity, question, or pain point. Encourage users to submit their ideas, collaborate to refine them, and vote on the most promising ones.

- Collect insights and data from all relevant stakeholders to evaluate the ideas. This step is crucial in determining the feasibility and potential impact of each idea.

- Conduct a thorough review to determine the final shortlist of ideas. Leverage the available data and insights to decide which ones to pursue for commercialisation.

- Implement a measurement and tracking system to monitor the performance of your innovation program. This will allow you to optimise your approach and ensure that you're meeting your goals.

- Reward the crowd so that the crowd does not get disillusioned.

Lean Management and Agile

Lean Management and Agile are proven methods of implementing projects that have direct applicability to the corporate innovators tool kit. Lean Management has its origins in the Toyota production system. It adopts a mindset of continuous improvement and flexible working processes in which all employees contribute new ideas. Lean organisations identify and eliminate activity that is not valued by the customer or end user. They use diagnostic tools such as root-cause analysis and value-stream mapping then implement improvements using management practices such as Kanban (a scheduling system) and/or Kaizen (a continuous improvement process). A systematic analysis of processes seeks to boost cost control, product quality, customer satisfaction, and employee engagement.

Agile is a more recent development that came out of the software industry. Rather than the traditional process of developing software solutions, Agile focuses on iterative development that puts a prototype into the customers' hands as quickly as possible. Agile teams then capture feedback and iterate via quick cycles, refining the solution over time. Agile's tools include the Stand Up (short, daily organisational meeting to agree and share priorities) and Sprints (a short, period when the team works to complete a set number of tasks). Scrums (team-based project management framework) are one of the more important implementation techniques.

A common misconception is that Lean Management and Agile are mutually exclusive. Lean is for routine tasks where continuous improvement is important. Agile is better suited to project or creative tasks. In reality, both share similar objectives and foundations: the desire to connect a goal to an outcome to give teams meaningful purpose; the importance of delivering value for the customer; and the desire to improve over time. Teams should therefore feel comfortable mixing and matching the tools depending on the circumstances.

Communication for a distributed workforce

Modern workforces are often distributed – even more so post-COVID. A major disadvantage of a distributed workforce is the loss of interpersonal communication; the advantage is that, correctly harnessed, it can lead to diverse thinking. The psychologist, Adam Grant, explains that he thought outstanding creative musicians, artists, scientists, and businessmen had a couple of big ideas they refined to perfection. However, the opposite is true. Throughout history, great thinkers do not have few ideas, they had lots of them, and much more than most of their peers.

Atlassian identifies the following useful lessons for handling communication in a distributed workforce. Do not limit the communication to just Zoom or email but introduce multiple platforms (like Slack and Trello), so each team member can find what suits their communication style best. Distributed work allows for a wider array of people to contribute. Pre-recorded videos with asynchronous feedback in a Google doc or Confluence page (on a deadline to ensure input) is one way to achieve this. Platforms like Confluence, Google Docs, and Trello can also help streamline innovation, alongside digital whiteboarding tools like Miro and Mural.

Implications

Companies need to review both the breadth of their training and use of innovation and collaboration tools. Helpfully, Gartner reviews and rates the best ones. There does not appear to be much research on their use in Australia. However, we do know that management capability is a critical driver of business performance and Australia is only in the second tier of countries in terms of the quality of its managers. Moreover, research quoted earlier has found that leading innovators use these tools more broadly than their less successful peers.

Most of the companies we interviewed used Agile for example, Fugro, Atlassian, RAC WA, Xero and so on. Major multinationals use a range of tools. For example, Woodside uses a range of processes to standardise its approach to innovation and accelerate the development of ideas to workable solutions. Agile technology development is used widely. Technology qualification is an approach to reduce the novelty risk in innovations. The company uses Lean Management and Six Sigma extensively, and a technology planning process clarifies what teams are working on and why. This enables comparisons, ensures alignment, and reduces overlap.

Key questions

- What tools are being used, and how effective are they in practice?

- If there are gaps, where are they and how can they best be filled?

- What additional measures could be taken to improve implementation planning?

Chapter 14

People and culture

People and culture are often identified as essential to innovation but represent the hardest area to change. The required change is less about formal training and more about developing the 'dynamic capabilities' to innovate successfully. Senior management must show commitment. Organisation structures must reflect that commitment, along with training, incentives, and governance processes. Finally, funds must be made available on a long-term basis.

Dynamic capability

Management capability is a critical driver of business performance. The United States, Sweden, Japan, Germany, and Canada have been identified as having the best managers, while countries like Australia, France, Great Britain, and Italy are in the second tier.[32] Australian organisations score highly in strategic management capabilities, but less so in adopting and integrating digital technologies and shifting towards environmental sustainability.

One key finding, is that most organisations are not aware of the quality of their own management or how to improve it.

Adopting best practices does not require innovation or new ideas; instead, organisations need to acquire and absorb the lessons that already exist. They need to measure and critically assess management practices, identify performance gaps, and initiate improvements.

In particular, they should develop dynamic capabilities which refers to an organisation's ability to adapt to changing circumstances and transform its business model and strategy to seize new opportunities or overcome challenges. These capabilities are essential in an environment where uncertainty and disruption are increasingly prevalent, and where the ability to act quickly and decisively is crucial for survival and success.

Dynamic capabilities include a range of skills and processes, such as sensing and seizing new opportunities, reconfiguring resources, and capabilities, and continuously learning and innovating. They require a long-term perspective, strategic thinking, and the ability to balance risk and reward. This is at the heart of the hackathon, accelerator, and corporate venturing. Having managers (at all levels) and decision makers participate in them is therefore vital for success.

Businesses that can develop and deploy dynamic capabilities are better positioned to respond to changing market conditions, customer needs and technological developments. They are also more likely to create sustainable competitive advantage that endures over time.

Senior management

A good proof point about a business's commitment to innovation is the amount of time senior executives spend on it. Whatever an organisation says about its commitment, if senior management are spending less than 20% of their time on innovation, it sends a message to employees that it is not important.

Leading organisations (for example, 3M and Alphabet) have institutionalised a percentage of time committed to innovation to emphasise that innovation takes place at all levels of the organisation. Atlassian's Product Security Team have taken this a step further. With COVID, the team found that staff were struggling to get the 20% free time to focus on innovation. Consequently, they created an Innovation Week every five weeks when the whole team pauses its regular work, forms ad-hoc teams and tackles different challenges.

A focus on innovation may mean not having a line responsibility at all. Proctor and Gamble (P&G) has a cadre of senior executives around the world to help identify promising innovation opportunities. These 'technology entrepreneurs', as the company calls them, are responsible for finding new ideas that can build on P&G's core businesses. The company credits its technology entrepreneurs with uncovering more than ten thousand potential offerings for review.

Finally, it means taking an honest look at the senior management and the board and asking whether they have the necessary expertise to make the required change. When a new CEO at BHP vowed to accelerate the group's adoption of technology, he added technology expertise to its board with the appointment of a former Hewlett Packard chief executive and a former SAP executive, the marvellously named, Xiaoqun Clever.

Structure

Organisational structure needs to reflect the innovation focus. We have already discussed the importance of innovation reporting to the CEO. Does the company's innovation function report to the CEO in your organisation or at least to a C-level executive? As companies grow, hierarchies proliferate – the old rule of no more than eight direct reporting staff ensures this will continue. However, it can be counter-productive to succeeding at innovation. The more hands and levels of approval a project needs to pass through, the greater the risk it can be watered down or ignored. Consulting group BCG has found that 'among companies that outperform their peers on innovation outcomes (as measured by their share of sales from new products and services), close to 90% demonstrate clear C-suite-level ownership, compared with only 20% of underperformers.'[33]

Amazon CEO Jeff Bezos has a two pizza rule: 'if a team can't be fed with two pizzas, it's too big.' Of course, the reality is more complex. However, research has found that while large teams are good at developing innovations, small teams can be critical for disruption. It is therefore important to examine the organisation structure and ask if it is innovation fit-for-purpose. Transformative innovations will often be better located and funded separately. Sustaining and adjacent innovations will probably be better housed and funded within the relevant business unit.

Several organisation structures are worth considering. A central R&D that covers both internal and external innovation will focus on short-term, incremental innovation and long-term transformative innovation within the same structure. Larger multi-divisional businesses may have within-unit R&D plus an innovation facilitation platform put in place by head office. This allows the division to determine the most appropriate type of innovation; however, head office may well provide a platform that crosses all the divisions, including training methodologies and approval processes. Finally, an independent innovation lab allows the organisation to demonstrate a separation from the core business to focus on innovation.

IAG initially chose the first option: bringing all its innovation initiatives into a single innovation and venturing hub. Operating across Australia, New Zealand, and Singapore, Firemark is made up of three functions: Futures, Ventures and Labs. Futures is a corporate research house. Ventures is the fund. Labs is akin to an accelerator that consists of a team of design, product, engineering, and business leaders that has been involved in, for example, Cyber360, a cyber self-defence platform for small to medium enterprises. Firemark identifies, invests in and incubates a portfolio of initiatives to accelerate new value creation within, and beyond, IAG's core insurance business. However, it retains links with the parent company and thirteen new technologies and data capabilities have been embedded in the parent, following successful internal trials. As we finalise this book, reporting for the innovation function has been folded into finance.

Graincorp has an executive responsible for innovation and growth within the business who reports to the CEO. Organic, digital innovations have their own teams and funding, with strong executive sponsorship. The venture fund is part of the same team. In contrast, innovation at Xero is spread across the executive team from the CEO to the chief strategy officer to the chief growth officer, because it is seen as everyone's business. Atlassian is the same.

The key is to find the structure that suits the organisation's strategy and not be sucked into simplistic solutions. For example, there is a myth about how flat structures decentralise authority by reducing hierarchy. They ought therefore to help organisations adapt better to changing environments.
However, instead of making managers obsolete, flat organisations may require even stronger management than hierarchical ones. With fewer managers, the span of control increases meaning they must delegate, monitor, and communicate across greater numbers of employees. Rather than being dynamic, managers with flat structures may end up making no decisions at all. A broader point is that flat structures may free staff up – but to do what? Studies show that even in start-ups, flat structures tend to be good at coming up with ideas, but they are less strong on delivering commercial outcomes.

While it makes sense to centralise innovation at the outset of an innovation journey, there is no one right structure. Each company must find a solution based on its unique circumstances and the changes it wants to make. Organisational structure, no matter how important, is only one tool to get the best from employees. SEEK is a great example. It was not the first to post classifieds jobs online in Australia, but it scaled better. The company was able to achieve this through centralized mass marketing and strategic alliances with companies like NineMSN and Telstra. By doing so, it outperformed established players who were keen to protect their legacy offline businesses.

Over the years, SEEK grew into new countries and markets. By 2021, the centralised structure was holding it back. It therefore decided on a new structure that would separate out its portfolio of start-ups into their own fund to provide greater focus and growth.

Trainings in a different way.

Staff and management ought to receive the appropriate amount of training to innovate successfully. That training needs to focus less on static knowledge and more on the dynamic capability. The 70–20–10 model of staff development holds that individuals obtain 70% of their knowledge from job-related experiences, 20% from interactions with others, and 10% from formal educational events. Participation in and exposure to hackathons, accelerators and corporate venturing is critical to learning hands-on skills or the dynamic capability referred to at the beginning of this chapter. The more staff that are involved in these types of activities the greater the individual benefit and flow on into culture change.

70-20-10 also tells us that strengthening management capability requires some formal training but plenty of hands-on experience. One of the most interesting examples is Mirvac's Hatch Innovation

Capability Accelerator (HICA). The international property group, Mirvac, has won awards for being an innovative place to work. HICA is designed as a school of innovation that supercharges the company's capability. Participants undergo an intensive training program in customer-centric innovation. They then apply their training directly onto their own projects. HICA alumni also drive foster cultural change across the company as a whole. So far, a quarter of Mirvac's workforce has been trained in HICA, and more than one hundred business projects have applied it to improve outcomes.

Governance and funding

Innovation projects, start-ups and innovative developments can be crushed if they are shoehorned in existing corporate processes. This is the challenge outlined in *The Innovator's Dilemma*. Innovation requires multiple small bets over long periods. As such, the standard credit committee processes to approve a new factory or mine or a major piece capital equipment are not appropriate to fund start-ups or innovations. Similarly trying to fit standard corporate supplier contracts to emerging companies does not work. Teams on the ground need to be delegated with the authority to make investment decisions within agreed limits, and budgets need to be set for the medium term rather than an annual basis.

In high-performing companies, innovation budgets are almost twice as likely to be funded by the business unit, as opposed to having a recurring corporate budget. Furthermore, organisations with a leading innovation capability are almost twice as likely to have iterative innovation budgets that are project based. This may sound contradictory, but the explanation is that innovative companies adopt a venture funding mentality. Incremental funding is unlocked on the achievement of clear milestones as well as supported by a suitable timeframe for implementation and growth.

Atlassian's Point A is a good example of a distributed approach to innovation. Atlassian wants the whole company to have the opportunity to contribute to collaborative innovation. The brand messaging consistently reinforces this: one of the company's core values is 'Be the change you seek'; even the ticker symbol (the unique series of letters assigned to a listed company for trading purposes) is TEAM.

Rewards, recognition, and incentives

A final proof point is rewards, recognition, and incentives. Whatever an organisation says about innovation, if the incentives are structured about cost reduction or short-term profit targets, employees would be remiss to do something else. Several of the organisations we interviewed used the OKR framework to align their teams. Objectives and Key Results is a goal-setting framework used to define measurable goals and track their outcomes. OKR's comprise an objective (a significant, concrete, clearly defined goal) and between three and five key results (measurable success criteria used to track the achievement of that goal). It is simple but powerful because it focuses on outcomes rather than more input-related measures such as time or investment.

Incentives should be structured to reflect the strategy and balance overall corporate objectives with what individual employees or teams can influence. Incentives do not need to be all financial; they may include reward experiences – days off, gift cards – or simply senior management or corporate-wide recognition. One of CSL's core values is innovation. It is also interesting that the technology businesses we spoke to all had at least one value around innovation or challenging the status quo. Performance against this value is explicitly discussed as part of employee appraisals. At Xero, for example, staff are reviewed annually via Xero-ins, and one of the core values built into our performance appraisal is innovation, called #challenge or think differently. Whatever level in the company, reviews at Xero stress that it is everyone's responsibility to help the company improve.

Culture as an output

> The crew's attachment to procedure instead of purpose offers a clear example of the dangers of prizing efficiency over adaptability.
>
> General Stanley McChrystal

By adopting these changes, organisations can develop the dynamic capability to succeed. Culture is an output of implemented changes, rather than something that the organisation tries to change in a vacuum. Innovative culture is not soft and informal, but the result of a disciplined approach. Businesses with an innovative culture combine several tensions: they tolerate failure but not incompetence; they experiment broadly in a focused manner; they are psychologically safe but candid; they have flat structures but are strongly led. These characteristics could almost define Moonshot Applied.

Reviewing people and culture means looking at where senior management spend their time, how the organisation and its innovation efforts are structured, trained, incentivised, governed and funded. Most employees are naturally innovative but require the right structure to do this successfully on a sustained basis. It is vital to examine the team to ensure the right skills exist, and we would highlight two areas for particular focus in terms of innovation. If the company has decided to set up a corporate venturing program, it is important to have someone with a background in venture capital. If the company is embarking on a Moonshot, the board needs to have someone who has experience of innovation, venture capital or technology to provide a knowledgeable voice.

Key questions

- How much time does senior management spend on innovation?

- How is innovation structured across the business and who does it report to?

- Is innovation included in the corporate training program?

- Is innovation governance and funding optimising outcomes?

- Are rewards, recognition and incentives, aligned to innovation?

- How are decisions made to stop projects not meeting their objectives?

Chapter 15

GOVERNMENT RESEARCH AND COLLABORATION

The final underpinning enabler used by leading innovators is government research and collaboration. Countries with high levels of innovation have a high degree of collaboration between industry, government, and research organisations. What is true of countries is also true of companies: leading innovators collaborate far more broadly than their less-successful peers. Australian government research entities and universities are world leaders in a number of areas. Organisations such as CSIRO and Cooperative Research Centres are tackling major issues, while bodies such the Australian National Fabrication Facility provide access to world-class testing labs and equipment. They have, and are continuing to evolve, programs to better support Australia's global innovation capability. Businesses looking to scale their innovation capability should therefore engage proactively.

Background

We noted earlier that Australia has only a mid-tier innovation track record. Too often local projects fail in the gap between basic research through to early-stage deployment and commercialisation. This is described as the 'valley of death', due to the numerous obstacles an innovation faces as it scales, such as running out of capital, staff burnout, lack of appropriate skills, access to customers or supplier delays.

Too often, a great idea does not make it to a great prototype, or a great prototype fails to be deployed commercially at sufficient scale to be successful.

Part of this inability to innovate at a country level is a structural failure of Australia's economy. Australia relies to a greater extent than many advanced economies on low complexity exports such as mineral resources. Mining and mining services have historically not involved significant R&D, when compared to industries such as manufacturing or pharmaceuticals. 'Collaborative Industry Research in Australia has been a partnership between research organisations and end markets,' says Adrian Beer from AIX. 'Companies that act as translation partners have not historically been involved in developing solutions and, as a result, research outcomes often fail to reach the wider market.' However, this trend is changing, and corporate innovation is increasingly flowing both into the resources industry and also across into other industry sectors such as defence, agriculture, and transport, and more recently, space. For example, Australia is building the Moon

Rover for the Artemis mission based on innovation proven in the remote, dusty, and difficult conditions of the Pilbara. That Moon Rover will be operated remotely from Australia using technology developed to operate subsea inspection robots one thousand metres underwater – not dissimilar to the communications signal issues the rover will face on the Moon.

Another aspect of this inability to innovate is historical. In the March 2017 financial quarter, Australia took the record for the longest run of uninterrupted GDP growth in the developed world. It was the one hundred and third quarter and the twenty-sixth year since the country had a technical recession. This does not lead to a massive desire for change.

Frontier innovation is the term economists use to refer to the first application of an innovation, while *catch-up innovation* refers to the application of an already existing innovation. A body of empirical evidence suggests Australia is behind the global innovation (or technology) frontier [34 and 35]. We have historically found it easier to adapt other country's innovations and, when they are locally developed, license or sell them to larger / more sophisticated foreign players to commercialise. The authors advocate companies not to give up on frontier innovation. Rather, they should look to collaborate and participate, notably with the deep resources available from government.

Governments invest in research and development. The most recent science, research and innovation budget tables show the Australian Government made a total R&D investment of $11.8 billion.[36] This includes university block grants provided by the Department of

Education and Training; competitive grants administered by the National Health and Medical Research Council and Australian Research Council, the Commonwealth Scientific and Industrial Research Organisation (CSIRO) and the Defence Science and Technology Group.

Collaborating or leveraging these resources is a powerful way to bridge the innovation valley of death. It means getting access to leading research, committed and deeply qualified resources and funding to ensure innovations have the broadest chances of success. A few highlights are provided below, outlining the main programs and a short section on New Zealand.

Figure 7 Think outside the bin

CSIRO

CSIRO, the Commonwealth Scientific and Industrial Research Organisation, holds the distinction of being Australia's national science organization and one of the world's largest and most diverse scientific research institutions. Its primary focus lies in tackling the nation's most pressing challenges, spanning areas such as space exploration, biodiversity preservation, food security, critical minerals, and oceanic studies, among others. Acting as a vital intermediary between scientific research and business, CSIRO aids Australian scientists in establishing their own enterprises while also enabling domestic companies to harness the power of science. With a presence across 55 sites in Australia and international locations like France, Chile, and the United States, CSIRO employs approximately 5,500 individuals.

CSIRO has recently assumed the role of Australia's largest data science group. It runs an accelerator program called ON, which offers invaluable support to research-driven start-ups. Through ON, CSIRO has assisted over 3,000 researchers in establishing more than 60 companies. These enterprises have collectively secured over $100 million in investment funding and a comparable amount in commercialization grants. CSIRO's commitment to fostering innovation is further exemplified by its Innovation Fund, Main Sequence Ventures, which focuses on translating Australian research into impactful companies that address significant challenges.

Over the years, Main Sequence Ventures has been instrumental in nurturing the growth of 42 deep technology companies and remains an early-stage meeting point for aspiring corporate innovators.

Business research programs

Successive Australian governments have developed an array of research-led, industry-led and government programs to facilitate and accelerate innovation. These will change over time, however the main ones are summarised below.

The Research and development tax incentive

The R&D tax incentive provides a way for companies to invest in R&D by alleviating key barriers that lead to underinvestment, such as not being able to capture the benefits of their R&D due to spillover effects and difficulty finding external finance.

Entrepreneurs' Program Innovation Connections

This provides support for companies concerning their competitiveness and productivity.

The Cooperative Research Centres (CRC) Program

The program partners industry with the research sector to solve industry-identified issues. For example, the Digital Finance CRC has $60 million funding to look at financial markets; in particular, the digitisation of assets so they can be traded and exchanged directly and in real-time. The SmartCrete CRC has $21 million in government funding to help develop the long-term viability of concrete infrastructure.

Imdex Case Study

Imdex, an ASX-listed engineering company that develops cloud-connected devices and drilling optimisation products, is a good example of how to collaborate with government. Technology leadership means targeted R&D. By and large, research is collaborative with third parties, especially universities and Cooperative Research Centres. Imdex works closely with CRC ORE and is also a key participant in MinEx CRC. Development is primary controlled in house, including a centre focused on sensor technology in California and another centre focused on BLAST DOG™ in Western Australia. (We discuss more about this innovation later.)

Industry growth centres

The centres identify knowledge priorities to inform researchers of industry needs. Growth centres directly assist industry and business to prosper by identifying priorities in key growth sectors, whereas CRCs undertake industry-focused research and development to address challenges requiring medium to long term research.

Examples of growth centres include METS (mining, equipment, technology and services) Ignited; NERA (National Energy Resources Australia); the Advanced Manufacturing Growth Centre (AMGC) and the Cyber Security Growth Centre (AustCyber). At the time of writing this book, no new funding was being made available for growth centres as the government reviewed its focus in this area.

Innovation precincts

Innovation precincts or clusters allow companies to better position themselves and accelerate cross-sector collaboration, targeted development, and innovation diffusion.

National Innovation Games

The games help find solutions to identified business challenges by connecting science, technology, engineering, and mathematics graduates with industry needs.

The Global Innovation Linkages and Global Connections Fund

The fund supports international collaboration on cutting-edge research translation and commercialisation projects. For example, the fund has provided a grant to an international consortium to support the clinical transition of a new-to-market diagnostic technology to improve cancer detection.

The ARC Industrial Transformation Research Program

The ARC seeks to attract both university-based researchers and companies. It funds research hubs and training centres while providing research students practical skills and experience through placement in industry.

State-based programs

For example, New South Wales is investing $360 million to deliver a Net Zero Industry and Innovation Program through high-emitting industries and the new low-carbon industry foundations focus areas.

New Zealand

Callaghan Innovation is New Zealand's innovation agency. Its objective is to enhance New Zealand's innovation ecosystem, working closely with government partners, Crown Research Institutes and other organisations that help increase business investment in R&D and innovation. This includes technology incubators, a product development accelerator, an innovation quarter, and ecosystem platform. R&D grants are available to complement the research and development tax incentive.

New Zealand Growth Capital Partners was established in 2002 to build an early-stage technology investment market. Its Aspire Fund invests directly into early-stage NZ tech start-ups alongside other like-minded investors. Its Elevate Fund invests into venture capital firms; aimed at filling the Series A and B capital gap for high-growth NZ tech companies.

Too little collaboration

We have discussed bringing outsiders in some type of competitive process to help generate and implement innovative ideas. Formal collaboration (notably with government) is another way of bringing greater breadth and scale to deliver innovation. It is a vital part of any company's innovation roadmap.

Australia does not collaborate well commercially. The Australian Bureau of Statistics (ABS) Business Characteristics Survey found only 14% of all companies, irrespective of industry or employment size, collaborated on innovation.[37] Among larger companies, this proportion was only slightly higher. Only 10% of Australian companies collaborated with universities or other higher education institutions. The main factors limiting collaboration were insufficient time and funds – yet those are the very levers from which well-planned collaboration will benefit. But it is not just about time and funding. Collaboration with organisations which have aligned goals provides a significant source of ideas, research, and innovation. It provides focus and processes to harness a wide array of resources to collaborate in solving difficult problems.

We have discussed the importance of diversity in decision making; indeed, the topic could be a book in itself. For this section, it is also important to note that collaboration drives diversity. Teams that include a wide range of ages, genders, backgrounds, and locations make better business decisions [38]87% of the time. Teams that follow an inclusive process make decisions two times faster with half the meetings.

CSIRO-UQ's Thriving Through Innovation survey found that leading companies collaborate broadly across stakeholder groups, including with suppliers and customers, as well as business research collaboration with university partners, public and private research organisations.[39] It was this breadth of collaboration that was the single clearest driver of performance. In terms of collaboration, leaders outperformed average-performing companies by eleven times! Kevin Dupe, Chairman Lifeline Direct, puts it more colloquially when he says organizations should 'keep the cupboard door open to others.'

The one caveat is that diversity, inclusivity, and collaboration must not compromise intellectual honesty. Innovation flourishes through debate and disagreement. While it is important to create an inclusive environment, it is equally important to create one where disagreement leads to greater knowledge. For example, when reviewing whether to move ahead with Amazon's Kindle, Jeff Wilke, the then CEO of Amazon's retail business, opposed the idea to the point that he challenged Jeff Bezos in a board meeting. Wilke predicted the company would miss its targets and frustrate clients because it was a software company that lacked experience in hardware. As Wilke recounts, his comments led to a more thorough discussion of the pros and cons of the decision, during which Bezos conceded Wilke's points but still argued that Amazon would be better served by developing a new set of skills. 'Turns out I was right on everything that I called out, and

Jeff was still right to say we should do it,' said Wilke. '[We] created a valuable skillset that we can use to invent new things on behalf of customers.'

The next section provides case studies on how leading innovators collaborate with government and other stakeholders.

Case Study: IMDEX BLAST DOG™

Commercial prototype IMDEX BLAST DOG™ was developed to provide near real-time blast hole physicals and orebody knowledge. It produces one thousand times the amount of data that would be available under traditional methods. The value of this knowledge is that it enables experts to make more informed decisions that affect each stage of the mining value chain. The BLAST DOG™ sensor is mounted on a tracked robotic platform with semi-autonomous hole positioning and alignment capability. Directly and rapidly measuring the orebody via blast holes reveals what the ore reserve looks like in the ground, at a high resolution, and immediately prior to its extraction, providing mining companies with insurance data that protects people, heritage, equipment, and neighbouring communities. The product originated out of informal discussions. It involved working with several Queensland-based small businesses for the delivery vehicle and advanced visualisation. Six years from conception, it is now being commercialised.

Case Study: CSL Incubator

CSL, the Walter and Eliza Hall Institute, and The University of Melbourne have joined forces to create an accelerator and commercial wet lab space for biotech start-up companies which will launch in 2024. The $95 million project is supported by the Victorian Government's Breakthrough Victoria Fund. It will be Australia's 'first and only' incubator co-located with a leading biopharmaceutical company, providing the corporate innovators with direct access to start-ups working on translating Australian medical research into new treatments and therapies.

> 'Formalising a place to nurture promising start-ups is a natural extension of our long-term support of, and collaboration with many like-minded partners. We hope to see significant long-term health, social and R&D benefits from this initiative, including greater retention and upskilling of domestic research and development capabilities and an increase in commercial acumen of [Melbourne Biomedical] Precinct researchers.'
>
> Dr Andrew Nash, Chief Scientific Officer and Senior Vice President, CSL Research

Case study: Woodside FutureLab

FutureLab is Woodside's innovation centre. The Woodside Monash Energy Partnership was launched in July 2019 as a multi-year research program to drive Australia's next generation of sustainable energy technologies and carbon solutions. Woodside is jointly investing $40 million over seven years to support projects in new energy technologies; carbon capture, conversion and utilisation; and energy leadership. A core team of three Woodside leaders and six Monash University researchers are leading the projects. Working with business partners and universities, FutureLab supports innovation with researchers, entrepreneurs, subject matter experts and parallel leading industries. Since FutureLab was established, it has connected dozens of new industry partners. It has also run hackathons areas associated with Woodside's core markets: additive manufacturing, data science and materials to fight corrosion.

Here to help

> The nine most terrifying words in the English language are I'm from the government and I'm here to help.
> President Ronald Reagan

Time and again we find companies underestimate the links between government and innovation. CSL, GrainCorp, and Telstra all originated from government investment. The encroachment of

Uber on the taxi industry shows that even if innovation is not directly subsidised or supported by government, it will often need to challenge or change government legislation or influence. Government's annual investment in R&D is over $11 billion. As this book goes to print, the Australian government is introducing a $15 billion National Reconstruction Fund and a Net Zero Authority to help manage the transition.

In other words, governments and research organisations are making significant efforts to support innovation, adapting their approach to be as relevant as possible. When the authors ask companies why they do not collaborate more, especially with government research, the answers are often rooted in a scepticism about the benefits, a concern with the extended time periods involved in getting agreement, cost overruns, and a fear of losing intellectual property. Very often, these criticisms do not apply to the way agencies work today. Even when they are valid, they can be overcome with a structured approach in almost all cases. In other words, the risks of working with government are far outweighed by the benefits. Globally, the evidence shows that more collaborative countries innovate more. And within Australia, top-performing companies collaborate more than worse performing ones.

Therefore, rather than blindly following Ronald Regan's dictum, any company looking to apply innovation to achieve a high impact should engage with government research. The nature of that collaboration will depend on the unique circumstances of the company and the industry in which it operates. For the moment, we will conclude by advising companies to take the time to find out how and what is on offer or engage with someone who has the networks and capacity to do that on their behalf.

> The federal government recently updated its list of Critical Technologies in the National Interest, some of which include AI, gene technology and vaccines, energy and environment, and robotics and space, and has earmarked AUD $1 billion to invest. But it's corporations that have a chance to make the biggest seachange. Government policy shouldn't be a benchmark to what the private sector spends. And we cannot rely on the public sector to lead the charge.
> Rohan Workman, CEO and Founder, Skalata Ventures

Key Questions

- Is the company's innovation strategy aligned to a sector-wide or national strategy?

- Is it aware of the government resources available to support research and development?

- How well does it collaborate with relevant government agencies on research?

- How well does it collaborate in general?

- Where and how could it do better?

PART THREE
NEXT STEPS

Chapter 16

Ambitious goals, outstanding implementation

Part Two outlined the key areas of the Ipsum innovation model. The thesis identifies where the company will invest its innovation dollars and why it believes it can succeed. Leading innovators are five times more likely to have a coherent investment thesis than their less successful peers. A portfolio review examines the composition and potential of the current innovations. Leading innovators commit twice as much of their innovation budget to transformational innovation when compared to their less successful peers. They are 60% more likely to use scaling processes – hackathons, accelerators and venture funds – to take ideas through to scale-ups. They generate twice the sales from new products and services. Underpinning these are tools to spot and develop winning ideas; to plan and manage implementation; to align people and culture; and collaborate with government research. Leading innovators are three times more likely to use tools like Open Innovation and eleven times more likely to collaborate externally than their less successful peers.

Part Three looks at next steps to create a Moonshot. Boards need to take a lead in challenging management around the innovation agenda.

Management needs to frame an appropriate response, including the goals, the actions supporting those goals, the timelines and resourcing. Leading innovators are five times more likely to have bold aspirations around innovation-led growth, and also match bold aspirations with tough choices.

The best place to start any innovation journey is the customer. Resource and structure the innovation function, so it is set up to succeed. Communication and training is paramount. Successful innovators supercharge their innovation pipeline with additional activities such as mergers and acquisitions.

Background

> There is nothing more difficult and dangerous, or more doubtful of success, than an attempt to introduce a new order of things.
>
> Niccolò Machiavelli, The Prince

Innovation is key to post-pandemic growth. Organisations that maintained their investment in innovation through the 2009 financial crisis outperformed the market average by more than 30% and continued to grow at a faster rate over the following three to five years.[40] Since then, the pace of change has only accelerated. Exponential technology is transforming markets. No company, sector or country will be untouched by the trillions of dollars that will be spent as we move to carbon neutrality.

Against this backdrop, businesses need to consider their innovation strategy and not be lulled into a false sense of security. Competitive advantage is temporary. In 2020, the average lifespan of a company on Standard and Poor's 500 Index was just over twenty-one years, compared with thirty-two years in 1965. As corporate longevity decreases, the ability to innovate at scale may be one of the few remaining sustainable advantages.

> The speed of technology change means that every company has an imperative for innovation. The balance between opportunity and risk may be different, as may organizational strengths and constraints. But no company will thrive if it does business in five years exactly the same way as it is doing business today. Customers expect more, and competitors will move faster.
> Ian Narev, CEO of SEEK Ltd, former Managing Director of Commonwealth Bank Group

It is therefore concerning to note that 87% of executives surveyed in the United States say innovation is one of their company's top priorities, but only one in five say they can innovate at scale. Paradoxically for many, the more obvious the need to innovate, the harder it can be to do it. An honest diagnostic of the company's innovation aspirations, practices and people is an important place to start. To get the right outcomes, this needs to involve senior management and the board.

> When the winds of change blow, some people build walls and others build windmills.
>
> Chinese proverb

Role of the board

The board of directors plays a vital role in driving innovation. It is a role that is primarily to test, question, and then ultimately support, or reject, ideas put forward by management. A recent study by the Australian Institute of Company Directors (AICD) and the University of Sydney found that while directors acknowledge the importance of innovation in their organisation's strategy, there are significant barriers preventing its effective implementation.[41] These include competing priorities, limited resources, and a lack of awareness of the need for change. This is a concerning result for corporate Australia. If businesses feel they have other priorities than creating their future, the obvious repost is to question what risk analysis has been used to come to this conclusion and what makes the company believe inaction is not riskier.

GrainCorp is a good example of how an established company can build on successful innovation. Their digital venture, CropConnect, is an online marketplace that offers a convenient and easy way to manage, sell and buy warehoused grain.

More than $4 billion worth of grain was transacted on the platform in 2022. A few years ago, GrainCorp ran a strategy session with the board of directors to build on the success of CropConnect and decided to accelerate its investment in innovation. They appointed a senior outsider to head their innovation function reporting to the CEO and launched GrainCorp Ventures (amongst other internal innovations) with a $30 million fund.

It is interesting to examine how the board of SEEK, one of Australia's leading innovators, approached a key decision around innovation. In 2021, the SEEK board completed an internal review and decided to place its early stage investment in a newly created SEEK Growth Fund. First, they created an independent board committee comprising four non-executive directors, an independent financial adviser and external legal counsel. Having concluded that the status quo was not optimal, they considered alternate options including an outright sale of the portfolio or having the portfolio managed by an external manager. The conclusion was that by 'far the best outcome for SEEK shareholders was for the existing team to manage the portfolio in a new highly aligned structure'. At the time of announcing the change, the company raised a significant amount of new capital into the Growth Fund.

The clarity and decisiveness of GrainCorp's and SEEK's board is unusual. The AICD study found that Australian directors believe they have low levels of innovation and digital literacy.

The top three AICD recommendations for the board were as follows:

- constructively challenge management and question long-standing assumptions on whether innovation is possible and its timeframe for implementation,

- ensure innovation is part of 'how we do business' in both the boardroom and the organisation,

- bring an 'innovation mindset' to board deliberations, while boards need to start hiring more directors with real-world innovation experience.

Innovation is still not a subject most boards discuss as a separate issue. In part this is because it is not well understood, but also because, for many board members and executives, it is seen as part of the way they do business. In this book, the authors have outlined a series of approaches for organisations to take to develop their innovation capability that is not part of the way most normally do business. We call it the Ipsum innovation model, and it represents a good way for boards to begin a conversation with management on innovation.

The importance of each area will change depending on the unique circumstances of the organisation. Nevertheless, the questions listed at the end of the book form a useful starting point, and the company can choose to dive more deeply into some areas than others.

Bold aspirations and tough choices

Exceptional leaders make tough choices to balance the short-term need for profits and the long-term need for innovation. For example, Netflix founder and CEO, Reid Hoffman, began to innovate around its core video rental business years before there was a burning platform. Xerox initiated an aggressive program to simplify its product set and reduce costs in its legacy business as it innovated in document management. Apple cannibalised its $5 billion per year iPod revenues by putting the whole mp3 player inside every mobile phone. However, one of the biggest gaps between innovation leaders and laggards is bold aspirations.

Leaders set aspirational goals and establish targets that rally talent to invent better ways to serve customers and society. Bold aspirations could be around a commitment to an innovative way of working. For example, 3M's Thirty Percent Rule, where 30% of each division's revenues must come from products introduced in the last four years, is tracked rigorously, and employee bonuses are based on successful achievement. At Google/Alphabet 10× thinking means thinking about something that is ten times better than existing options.

Bold aspirations are commonly around an investment of capital. Telstra Ventures latest Fund III is $350 million. GrainCorp has made a $30 million investment in GrainCorp Ventures. CSL has announced a $95 million investment in its accelerator. Woodside has set aside $5 billion to invest by 2030 in line with a global push for cleaner energy. Woodside is focused on producing the new energy, lower carbon, and carbon solutions, required by their customers, like hydrogen and ammonia opportunities, while continuing to supply affordable, reliable, and lower carbon, liquefied natural gas (LNG).

At the outset, any bold aspiration is likely to be measured by inputs. This seems modest. However, too often, companies claim they want to innovate but do not provide the resources to make that innovation successful. Innovation on a scale that will make a meaningful impact to a large company requires resources deployed at scale. Moving from inputs to outputs is difficult. For example with Woodside, while individual innovation projects have targets, budgets and timelines, there are not specific measures for the contribution of innovation overall. This is in part because the timescales can be long, but more importantly, if the innovations are successful, they will often be folded into the main business. Woodside was instrumental in getting new ships to use LNG. As of 2023, around 30% of the new large-size vessel orders are fuelled by LNG. This is the result of a decade of work.

Finally, ambitious goals force businesses to attempt innovative approaches which would not be attempted if we were only aiming at incremental improvement. They create urgency and hold the organisation to account if it does not deliver. This means challenging assumptions and thinking outside the box to identify innovative solutions that can be achieved through rapid experimentation and iteration. However at some point, ambition needs to translate into implementation.

From ambition to implementation

Australian biotech company CSL typifies how to translate ambition into implementation. CSL was founded in 1916 as the Commonwealth Serum Laboratories, an Australian Government body focused on vaccine manufacture. In 1994, it was privatised and listed on the Australian stock market. Its strategy has been to hire star scientific talent, invest heavily in research and development, protect intellectual property, and enter into strategic alliances to fill resource gaps. In terms of innovation, CSL runs its Research Acceleration Initiative to fast-track discovery of biotherapies through partnerships between CSL and global research organisations. It also has an AI Centre of Excellence comprising dozens of data scientists.

Leaders in various parts of the company who are interested in launching AI initiatives consult the data science team to learn about best practice. Simultaneously, CSL pursues an acquisition strategy to fill gaps in its portfolio.

The company has an R&D pipeline of about sixty drugs from Phase I through to Post-Registration. Each is classified by the strategic platform (for example, Gene and Gene Therapy) and therapeutic area (for example, immunology or haematology). The highly regulated nature of pharmaceutical approvals makes it easier for CSL to do this. However, other companies could learn from this transparency. CSL's R&D is split out into New Product Development (activities that focus on innovative new therapies for life-threatening diseases); market development (strategies that seek to bring therapies to new markets and new indications); and life cycle management (ensures continuous improvement of existing products). It also monitors external innovator engagement including partnerships with universities, direct investments in venture capital and its accelerator. Over the past five years, CSL's share price has outperformed the ASX by four times!

From implementation to transformation

Eagle-eyed readers will have noted that we have almost got through a book on innovation with minimal use of the dreaded word, transformation. Transformation is over-hyped and too often has come to describe an IT project. What it does do is capture the scale of changes required to deal with the trifecta of technology blurring of markets, exponential growth, and business model disruption. Transforming at either the project or company level requires not just the ambitious goals but a structured approach to achieving them.

At its core, we argue that sustained innovation is less about creative ideas and more about resource allocation and alignment. Leading companies align people, processes, and resources to succeed at scale. They use some version of hackathons, accelerators, and corporate venturing. They sustain their efforts by underpinning these processes with best practice tools. Of course, less innovative companies use each of these as well, but it is striking how leading innovators use them more and with greater depth than their less successful peers. The result is Jim Collins' flywheel where effort is required to get innovation moving, but with each turn, it becomes easier, and momentum builds.

For leading innovators, this momentum is harnessed to generate more energy and drive the flywheel faster.

No company exists in a vacuum, and it is important to consider whether your innovation strategy is aligned to a sector wide or national strategy. The key is to ensure that effort is not duplicated, collaboration is maximised, and the company sets itself up to succeed, given the significant sector wide resources available to support innovation. For example, the winners of the Charge on Innovation Challenge get to work with BHP, Rio, Vale and sixteen other miners to accelerate the commercialisation of interoperable solutions to safely deliver electricity to large battery electric off-road haul trucks.

Looking at the company's strategy within the context of government and the market sector helps to unpick what is required to develop innovations at scale. Xero accounting software may not seem to need to be close to government, but it is hugely affected by how government mandates companies and individuals prepare their tax returns. Consequently, it needs to work closely with governments across the different countries in which it operates to help understand and get approval for innovations.

Key issues to get right

The IPSUM innovation model provides a systematic way to approach reviewing and developing an innovation strategy. However, when we asked the interviewees what advice they would give to companies looking to improve their innovation on top of this model, the following areas were most often cited.

Start with the customer

SEEK starts by asking if the proposed solution trying to solve problems for job seekers and hirers. If not, 'it's just novelty.' Every company and individual we have interviewed for the book has said something similar. Customer-facing innovation forces the company to look outwards, stands a higher probability of delivering sales, and protects the core business. NAB Ventures invests in businesses that help their customers better manage their financial needs, support them through the home ownership journey, facilitate better payments and/or build wealth for them. Xero has customer excellence centres and executives clock in once a year to hear what issues our customers are facing and how our staff are dealing with them. Amazon is famous for its focus on the customer. In his 2002 letter to shareholders, Jeff Bezos noted that the 'American Customer Satisfaction Index gave the company a score of eighty eight, the highest customer satisfaction score ever recorded in any service industry, online or off. A representative was quoted as saying, *If they go any higher, they will get a nose bleed*. We're working on that.'

Resource and structure innovation

Do this so it can occur at the same time as business as usual. Corporate executives must manage today's products and processes, while also laying the groundwork for the innovations that will define the future. To do that sustainably and at scale requires different processes, structures, and cultures. Simultaneously, the best companies maintain capability links across units at the senior executive level. In other words, business as usual recognises the need to innovate and innovation recognises the need for business as usual. This has been called the ambidextrous organisation.

SEEK set up its Growth Fund containing a number of early-stage investments and the more mature, Online Education Services. As SEEK said at the time: 'Greater independence and focus have led to the seeded assets adopting more aggressive re-investment strategies that were harder to implement under the prior operating model.' The internal valuation of the Seek Growth Fund rose 38% in its latest stock exchange filings.

UBank is an Australian direct bank owned by NAB. NAB realised that many younger clients did not identify with Australia's big four banks. Digital-only fintechs had been successful globally. They had a lower cost base and could offer selected products at better returns than their integrated competitors. From the perspective of UBank, NAB was able to deliver a banking licence, balance sheet, risk management and technology infrastructure. From the perspective of NAB, UBank was able to pilot a range of innovations without risk to the main brand. In 2019, Ubank introduced the world's first digital human, named Mia, aimed at helping home buyers apply for their home loans. This innovation aimed to disintermediate mortgage brokers and their businesses. Not all UBanks innovations have been successful, and the company has ceased offering new accounts and term deposits for self-managed super funds. Nevertheless, NAB's structuring and resourcing of this innovation has been critical to its success.

Resource allocation links both these examples. In both cases, innovation is separate from but linked to the core business to succeed, and both are enabled with the right level of resources: financial, management and capabilities.

Success Measures

Any well-managed innovation process includes mechanisms to track ongoing initiatives and ensure they are progressing according to plan. Companies typically rely on stage-gate processes to assess projects periodically, recalculate their projected returns according to any changed conditions, and decide whether they should get a green light to move onto the next phase. This works for sustaining and adjacent innovations which operate to a predictable funnel. However, transformative innovations may require more time and a more flexible approach. As discussed earlier, they may require some explicit acceptance of the value non-financial success measures such as exploration and learning. Above all, the use of hackathons, accelerators and corporate venturing provides a proven pathway to develop and scale the innovation pipeline.

Communication and training

Everyone we have spoken to has also told us not to underestimate the effort and energy required to change culture. Change must be demonstrated at every level in an organisation and executives must be seen to support and promote it.

It is easy to lose momentum as executives return from another innovation program which has taken up a significant amount of time and appears to have made only a few trivial steps towards solving a problem. It is easy to imagine time would be better spent meeting customers, reviewing staff performance, or writing board papers rather than mentoring one of the projects or start-up cohorts from an accelerator or other aligned initiative. The key point is that applied innovation is the future of any organisation and must receive top-down support and championing to maintain momentum. Understood correctly, the hackathon and other such events serve several purposes: developing specific innovations; giving management the dynamic capabilities to innovate repeatedly; and sending a signal to employees and the industry on the importance the company places on innovation.

Supercharge innovation

High-growth companies pursue innovation to deliver better financial or customer outcomes, rather than the defensive reason of simply cutting costs. Correctly managed, *Moonshot Applied* supercharges the innovation pipeline from problem identification to deployment. By adopting these processes at scale, organisations create a valuable future.

The final point about implementation is that it must involve meaningful capital investment to deliver meaningful results which does not stop when the innovation has reached maturity.

This can be achieved organically. For example, CSL and Telstra have significant global resources (customers, sales, partners) to accelerate the roll out of new pharmaceuticals or technology products.

Atlassian has a global platform to layer on new products for software developers, project managers and other development teams. However, in most cases, growth is also accelerated via M&A. For example, CSL has an outstanding track record of using M&A to fill gaps in its portfolio and accelerate growth, Atlassian has the same.

Chapter 17

MAKING IT STICK

Moonshot Applied is a term for the way leading companies innovate repeatedly at scale by combining bold ambition with outstanding implementation. It is an optimistic alternative to cost cutting yet only a few manage to make it stick. Psychological studies show we make a greater effort to avoid painful experiences than enjoy pleasurable ones. Worse still, we find it easy to learn from our successes but are poor at learning from our failures. Leading organisations use these biases to reinforce rather than shy away from innovation. In the main, they develop solutions to create an innovative culture rather than the other way round. And finally, they see innovation as the engine that creates the company's future.

> The creaky old wheels of our commodities-based economy are slowly turning towards knowledge, innovation, and invention. The mixing of inventive genius with business brilliance is indispensable if we want to compete with other advanced economies. As the law of accelerated returns tells us, growth in knowledge

and understanding is always exponential. The longer we languish, the more we fall behind.

Rohan Workman, CEO and Founder, Skalata Ventures

Biases

At the beginning of this book, we say that corporate innovation is turning ideas into profitable solutions that add value to customers. Rather than being about creativity, innovation is about resource allocation and only a few businesses manage to align their people, processes, and resources to succeed at scale. *Moonshot Applied* companies move faster. From the first meeting with Steve Jobs where he outlined iTunes to Jeff Bezos, Amazon took four years to launch the Kindle.

Competitions are a way to source and combine ideas quickly from different sources. The adoption of software planning techniques like agile ensures leading companies rapidly prototype then iterate, rather than spending too much time planning and approving. It means they overcome cognitive biases and have a different attitude to risk and failure.

We regularly use the spaghetti marshmallow challenge as a team-building exercise to demonstrate these concepts in action. This challenge showcases how preconceptions can limit our ability to think outside the box and find creative solutions. It also highlights the benefits of rapid prototyping and iteration, which are essential in the innovation process. The challenge involves building the tallest freestanding structure that can support the weight of one marshmallow, using only twenty sticks of spaghetti, a yard of string, strips of scotch tape, and a single marshmallow. Teams have only eighteen minutes to create a structure that can hold the marshmallow, which emphasises the importance of prototypes and iterations in the innovation process.

This exercise has been used in various settings, including Fortune 500 companies, exclusive business universities, and local schools and nurseries for young children. It is a valuable tool for teaching applied innovation processes because it emphasises the need for rapid prototyping and iteration to arrive at the best solution. Interestingly, MBA students often perform poorly as this challenge, while kindergarteners tend to excel. This is because children are less risk-averse and more willing to experiment and try new things without hesitation, which is a crucial aspect of applied innovation.

While most executives know the importance of innovation, it is extraordinarily difficult to change behaviour. Business as usual invariably seems more pressing and more real than innovation which is inherently uncertain and may take years to come to fruition. Psychologists call this the intention–action gap. Most adults know exercise is good for them and would like to do more, yet global studies have shown that up to 55% of people never manage to convert intention into action.

Before we get too despondent, it is worthwhile pointing out that psychology can also provide us with tools to compensate for cognitive biases and overcome the intention-action gap. This involves seeking outside perspectives and having the courage to accept volatility.

It means keeping innovations separate from business as usual but maintaining tight links between them. We looked at how the venture capital mindset differed from the standard corporate mindset and how they obtained outsized returns from a tiny proportion of their investments. Leading corporate innovators have a similar mindset: they are more outward-looking in terms of where they source innovations; they are more likely to focus their innovation efforts on solving customer problems; and they collaborate more with third parties.

Habits bridge the intention – action gap

Leading companies make small, repeatable experiments in innovation supported by a proven toolset. In short, they make innovation a corporate habit. Psychology tells us that to become ingrained habits need cues, repetition, and rewards.

We have discussed hackathons and accelerators and suggest these form cues that signal to employees the importance of innovation to the organisation. Use of hackathons and accelerators needs to be repeated and there needs to be rewards that can be both monetary and non-monetary. Atlassian's use of them for almost twenty years has created a long list features and internal programs that have become part of the company folklore.

Ensure a stable environment

The average life of a corporate venturing program is four years when means the vast bulk are much shorter. Employees want to learn and will take the time to develop new behaviours provided they think management is serious. However, too often, innovation budgets are cut when the going gets tough. One of the most important things an executive and board can do therefore is ensure a stable environment for employees to learn by committing to innovation over the long term. Six years from conception, Imdex is now commercialising BLAST DOG™. Telstra's accelerator program Muru-D is a decade old. Atlassian's commitment to decentralised innovation has been part of the company's culture from the outset.

Leverage a disruption of the status quo

When J. F. Kennedy gave his Moonshot speech, he deliberately put it in the context of competing against Russia. While a stable commitment is important, to get the best impact it should be done against a backdrop of disruption and threat. The Charge On Innovation Challenge large battery electric off-road haul trucks is a great example of a disruption to the status quo: the net zero is so great that mining competitors are willing to work together to find a solution.

Building on what is great in the company, piggyback on an existing habit

Significant change in an individual or organisation is very rare. Approaches which bolt a new behaviour on to an existing one can be more effective than starting from scratch. When David Thodey launched Telstra Ventures, he focused on leveraging the telecommunication giant's customers rather than its technology.

This cleverly side-stepped the pitfall of being too inward-looking and sent a strong message to Telstra's employees about what made the company great.

Eliminate friction

A further lesson from psychology is to eliminate friction to make habit forming as easy as possible. The easier the setup, the more likely we will at least start the new behaviour. SEEK, Xero and Atlassian stop work to run their hackathons, yet too often we see other companies run hackathons on weekends, so they do not eat into work time. Too often a commitment to innovation (for example, 20% of time dedicated to it) is abandoned to meet a deadline or undermined by incentives and targets that are focused on business as usual. For Woodside, innovation is not an elective. It is a given like safety and diversity. Increasingly therefore, the company is looking to have innovation as part of a distributed culture to 'Innovate Every Day'.

CSL's incubator is located in its own head office to provide corporate innovators with direct access to start-ups working on translating Australian medical research into new treatments and therapies, and start-ups direct access to decision-makers.

Need for speed

The combination of stability plus a burning platform and eliminating friction is the ability to move fast. In research quoted earlier, fast moving companies innovated at almost 5x the speed of their slower peers. Of course, it is not innovation for innovation's sake, rather it is innovation within an investment thesis using the scaling processes and underpinning enablers covered earlier in the book. One of the interviewees starts his senior management meetings with the phrase: 'first be nimble'.

Stay optimistic

We said earlier that *Moonshot Applied* is an optimistic approach that focuses on the company's ability to innovate, rather than defend business as usual. When faced with the threat of climate change, BHP's vision remains to build a better world. When faced with the existential threat of iTunes, Amazon's response was to create an entirely new market category in Kindle. Instead of finding reasons to say no, innovation is about saying, 'What can go right?' Contrary to 'If it ain't broke don't fix it', it is about seeing an improvement and then seeing ways to improve the improvement.

Rather than looking for consistency of outcome, innovation recognises that wins will be irregular, but they can also be transformative.

> The possibilities that lie in the future are infinite. When I say 'It is our duty to remain optimists,' this includes not only the openness of the future but also that which all of us contribute to it by everything we do.
>
> Karl Popper

Solutions first, culture second

We are entering a period of exceptional risk and opportunity so there has never been a more important time to look at innovation-led growth. As Warren Buffet once said: 'Cash combined with courage in a crisis is priceless.'

Rather than trying to undercut the competition, innovation leaders strive to anticipate the needs of their customers and make the competition irrelevant. Beyond that, to innovate repeatedly at scale companies must adapt a strategy to their own unique circumstances. Part will be determined by the industry, the customers, and the unique resources and assets a company can bring to innovation.

Some innovation programs focus on changing culture first, whereas others focus on finding customer solutions. Culture-led programs tend to focus on incremental, rather than transformative innovation.

They will be more internally focused when looking for sources of new ideas and developing a decentralised innovation capability. The innovations will tend to be sustaining rather than transformative. For example, Xero does not use the term much because innovation is ingrained in the culture. Atlassian is very publicly committed to a decentralised innovation because it 'is everyone's job – from the CEO to the intern who started last week. That's a radically different mindset from relying on the creativity of a (mythical) lone genius, and it comes with equally radical implications'.[42] The company has even published a no-BS guide to building a culture of innovation which is well worth a read.

Atlassian, SEEK and Xero are exceptions, notably in Australia, in that they are technology companies disrupting global marketplaces. Working with local companies for more than a decade, the authors believe that to succeed most organisations should not start internally with culture. The management guru, Peter Drucker, once wrote that culture ate strategy for breakfast. However, in the authors' experience, Australian companies are more likely to be successful if they focus externally on transformative innovation that solves specific customer problems through a centralised function. Once this has demonstrated progress, broader culture change follows as a matter of course.

Faced with declining sales, Xerox began an aggressive program to simplify its product set and reduce costs. At the same time, it began innovating. The rise of the internet meant less demand for physical printing and copying. However, those same forces opened up a new opportunity for office automation.

Having developed solutions organically, Xerox acquired Affiliated Computer Services Inc. (ACS), a company specialising in business process automation. Three years later, Xerox had recovered the sales it had lost and created significant value for shareholders. However, no change lasts for ever, and a number of years after that Xerox decided to split the business into the old copying and process automation lines.

Concluding thoughts

> Every morning in Africa, a gazelle wakes up. It knows it must run faster than the fastest lion or it will be killed.

> Every morning a lion wakes up. It knows it must outrun the slowest gazelle or it will starve to death. It doesn't matter whether you're a lion or gazelle. When the sun comes up, you'd better be running.

Whether they work for incumbent lions or start-up gazelles, hard-headed managers face difficult market conditions with customers and suppliers wanting better deals, pressure on costs just as profits are threatened, and nervous shareholders. At best, growth and innovation can seem fluffy and uncertain in this environment. At worst, it appears to be a distraction from the hard stuff of management, business as usual.

Moonshot Applied has made the case a different approach. The world's best-performing companies compete based on innovation. In most cases, growth is a stronger driver of shareholder value than improving margins. Two companies featured in this book as leading innovators – CSL and Cochlear – are amongst the top three performing stocks in the ASX over the past decade.

Successful corporate innovators craft a vision that contains practical pathways to success including specific, ambitious goals linked to societal benefit, and breakthrough technology selected via competition. Then, they align people and resources to implement at scale. The book's title tries to embody this combination of bold vision and superb implementation.

Moonshot Applied is founded on the belief that abundant opportunities exist for businesses and society, provided they learn from the way leading companies approach innovation. It is not a soft skill but a hard discipline that requires time and effort to master. International and domestic examples demonstrate it is less about creativity and more about resource allocation and processes such as the hackathon, the accelerator and corporate venturing.

Over the coming decades, trillions of dollars will be invested on the net zero transition. In today's rapidly changing business landscape, the ability to respond to and leverage disruption is essential for long-term success. Atlassian emphasises the importance of 'enabling scalable, distributed innovation that can match or beat the pace of the rest of the company's growth'. To achieve this, companies must generate, test and scale ideas faster than the pace at which external factors are changing.

Many Australian companies need to change. The path to success is not easy, and the rewards will only be shared among a select few. This is not only due to the inherent risks involved in innovation, but also because laggards are playing catch up while leading innovators are continually improving. It is not surprising they outperform the index by 30%, while non-innovators trail by 120%.

To succeed in innovation, businesses must be bold and ground their ideas in their unique circumstances. They must view themselves, at least partially, as venture capitalists and technology companies. By learning from the former, they can identify and scale innovation effectively. By learning from the latter, they can harness society's most potent change engine to solve customer problems. Sun Tzu in the *Art of War* reminds us that success is as much about internal self-knowledge as external insight, 'if you know the enemy and you know yourself, you need not fear the result of a hundred battles'.

Most important of all, companies must believe that innovation is not a distraction from business as usual, it is the engine creating the company's future.

> We've had three big ideas at Amazon that we've stuck with for eighteen years, and they're the reason we're successful: Put the customer first. Invent. And be patient.
>
> Jeff Bezos

Ipsum innovation model questions

Companies wanting to sustain exceptional innovation at scale need to learn from the best. The Ipsum innovation model provides a comprehensive approach about what leading innovators do different from their less successful peers. Not all areas of the model will be equally relevant, but the following questions provide an excellent place to start.

Investment Thesis

- Does the company have an explicit innovation strategy setting out where innovation fits into the overall strategy with quantified and funded targets?
- Has it mapped the relevant exponential technologies across the value chain?

- Has it discovered the business models to commercialise these technologies and their potential impact on the market?

- Has it developed a thesis about where the company will focus its investment and the 'secret sauce' or unique insights it could expect to bring to give it a higher probability of success?

- What are the gaps between its current strategy and the above questions?

Innovation portfolio:

- Does the company have an innovation portfolio?

- How well is it managed and has it grown in value?

- What is its composition (sustaining, adjacent, transformational) and potential (value and business benefit)?

- Is there a gap between the aspirations, investment thesis and portfolio, and what are the appropriate actions to close it?

Scaling processes – hackathons:

- Does the company use hackathons systematically and for a clear purpose?

- How extensive is the effort to ensure suitable participants?

- Is there a defined process to support solutions developed through the hackathon?

- Have the winning ideas been celebrated, carried forward and the outcomes measured?

- Do key executives participate?

- What are the outcomes? Have they met stated objectives?

- How could they be improved?

Accelerators:

- Is the company involved in internal and/or external accelerators and if not why?

- How does it engage with participants and how do its staff and participants benefit?

- What has been the outcome in terms of working with and or investing in start-ups?

- What is in place to ensure rapid development of solutions beyond the accelerator?

- How could it be improved?

Corporate venturing:

- How effectively does the company fund the growth of its portfolio of innovations?

- How does it tap into external markets trends and early disruptors?

- Does the company have a clear idea of how it could successfully launch and sustain a corporate venturing initiative?

- How could it improve?

Underpinning enablers – winning ideas:

- Does the company have an approach to recognising and evaluating winning innovation ideas?

- What are the lessons in terms of how successful this has been?

- How deeply ingrained are these lessons in the company's culture?

- How aligned are the winning idea with the over-arching company strategy and investment thesis?

Implementation planning:

- What tools are being used and how effective are they in practice?

- If there are gaps, where are they and how can they best be filled?

- What additional measures could be taken to improve implementation planning?

People and culture:

- How much time does senior management spend on innovation?

- How is innovation structured across the business, and who does it report to?

- Is innovation included in the corporate training program?

- Is innovation governance and funding optimising outcomes?

- Are rewards, recognition and incentives aligned to innovation?

Government research:

- Is the company's innovation strategy aligned to a sector-wide or national strategy?

- Is it aware of the government resources available to support research and development?

- How well does it collaborate with relevant government agencies on research?

- How well does it collaborate in general?

- Where and how could it do better?

Moonshot:

- What are the goals?

- What are the actions supporting these goals?

- What are the timelines?

- What is the resourcing (people, process and financial)?

About the Authors

In the dynamic realm of corporate innovation and leadership advisory, the experience and combined expertise of seasoned professionals Brett Savill and Peter Rossdeutscher are both rare and invaluable. Their careers are marked by significant contributions and impact, positioning them as thought leaders and sought-after advisers.

Brett and Peter have amassed a wealth of knowledge while nurturing a profound understanding at the Board and Executive level in applying innovation models to all types of organizations. As authorities in strategy-focused innovation, they offer a perspective that encompasses corporate culture, venture capital, entrepreneurial ecosystems, and R&D.

Their insights provide actionable strategies that serve as indispensable guides in the complex journey of navigating the corporate landscape, offering clarity and direction in the pursuit of innovation and business success. With a shared commitment to driving positive change and a proven track record of transformative leadership, these models have been adapted to meet the rapidly changing market demands of technology and sustainability.

Brett Savill's introduction to innovation came when he helped Intel Capital at PricewaterhouseCoopers (PwC). Plus working with start-ups, he is an experienced executive, non-executive director, and adviser in the corporate, government and not-for-profit sectors. Brett has been a CEO, COO, CFO, and corporate development director. He is also a former PwC partner and senior adviser at Alvarez and Marsal, as well as Chair of leading addiction charity, SMART Recovery Australia. He has a BA (Hons), MBA, and is a Fellow of the Australian Institute of Directors. In his spare time, he plays golf badly and writes fiction.

Peter Rossdeutscher is an independent Board Director, former Global Managing Director, Philanthropist and Adviser on digital innovation, commercialisation leadership, and tackling social inequities. He led significant global companies in Asia and Australia, including MD of Gateway Asia and CEO of Australian unicorn, Micromine. His commitment to positive change has been recognised by being awarded ICT Achiever of the Year and a Finalist for the Champion of Mining Technology Innovation. He cofounded the not-for-profit initiatives First Nations X and Quantum Girls. Peter has been an Adjunct Professor of Innovation and Entrepreneurship, is a Fellow of the Australian Institute of Company Directors, Companion of the Institute of Engineers Australia and INSEAD International Certified Director.

LISTS OF FIGURES AND TABLES

Figures

Figure 1. Ipsum innovation model 4
Figure 2. Sustaining Vs Transformational 12
Figure 3. Venture capital return on investment risk asymmetry 42
Figure 4. Too little transformation 85
Figure 5. Moonshot scaling processes 94
Figure 6. Our innovation process 143
Figure 7. Think outside the bin 185

Tables

Table 1. Ipsum innovation model components 65
Table 2. Financial and Non-Financial Metrics 154
Table 3. Stage Development Valuation 158

Acronyms and abbreviations

ABS   Australian Bureau of Statistics
ACS   Affiliated Computer Services Inc.
AICD   Australian Institute of Company Directors
AMGC   Advanced Manufacturing Growth Centre
AP&A   Asia Pac and Americas
ASX   Australian Stock Exchange
AUV   autonomous underwater vehicle
AWS   Amazon Web Services
BCG   Boston Consulting Group
BHP   Broken Hill Proprietary
CBA   Commonwealth Bank of Australia
CSIRO   Commonwealth Scientific and Industrial Research Organisation
CSL   Commonwealth Serum Laboratories
DNA   deoxyribonucleic acid
EBIT   earnings before interest and taxes
ESG   environment social and governance
FMG   Fortescue Metals Group
GDP   gross domestic product
HICA   Hatch Innovation Capability Accelerator

IAG Insurance Australia Group Limited
ICT information and communication technology
IEA International Energy Agency
INSEAD Institut Européen d'Administration des Affaires (European Institute of Business Administration)
IP intellectual property
IPO initial public offering
ITDs Intel Capital Technology Days
LED light-emitting diode
LNG liquefied natural gas
M&A mergers and acquisitions
MAYA most advanced yet acceptable
METS mining, equipment, technology and services
NAB National Australia Bank
NASA National Aeronautics and Space Administration
NASDAQ National Association of Securities Dealers Automated Quotations
NERA National Energy Resources Australia
NZ New Zealand
OECD Organization for Economic Co-operation and Development
OKR Objectives and Key Results framework
PwC PricewaterhouseCoopers
R&D research and development
SME small and medium-sized enterprises
TAM Total Addressable Market
TRL technology readiness level
UTS University of Technology Sydney

ACKNOWLEDGEMENTS

This book would not have been possible without the achievements of countless individuals in start-ups, angel investors, small-to-medium enterprises, multinationals, entrepreneurs, venture capitalists, government departments, universities and agencies, who work on innovations every day. We are mindful of Winston Churchill's dictum that criticism is easy, but achievement is hard. We would like to single out and thank the following contributors, listed in alphabetical order:

Dr James Arvanitakis, Director, Forrest Research Foundation.
Matthew Ayres, MD, Growth and Innovation Asia Pacific.
Adrian Beer, Managing Director, Australian Innovation Exchange.
Emeritus Professor David Blair, The University of Western Australia.
Alan Bye, MD, Imvelo. Former Vice President Technology, BHP.
Paul Cheever, Chief Executive, Australian Institute for Innovation.
Peter Clarke, Principal, Innovation Consulting Australia.
Clytie Dangar, Global Head of Partnerships, Imdex.
Kevin Dupe, Chairman, Lifeline Direct.
James Edwards, GM Innovation, Royal Automobile Club of WA.
Heidi Edwards, GM Knowledge and Innovation, Rio Tinto.
Sarah Endacott, Editor.
Barry Fitzgerald, CEO, Roy Hill.
Sam Forbes, Director, SpAARC.
Sharna Glover, Co-Founder, Imvelo.
Tom Goerke, Managing Director, Trestle Digital
Justin Hillier, Chief Commercial Officer, Essential Energy.

Graeme Houston, former GM, Yum! Restaurants International.
Neil Kavanagh, Chief Scientist, Woodside Energy.
Susan Kreemer Pickford, General Manager, WA Engineers Australia.
Alice Manners, Chief Customer Officer, Brightwater Care Group.
Dr Kent Matla, Managing Partner, Triangle Equity Partners.
Aaron Michie, Head of Marketing, Ops, Strategic Programs and Transformation, Foxtel Group.
Kylah Morrison, GM Skills and Innovation, METS Ignited.
Ian Narev, Chief Executive Officer, SEEK.
Dan Ratner, Chief Executive Officer, Uberbrands.
Greg Reibe, Principal, Entrepreneurs in Residence.
Peggy Renders, CCO, Enterprise & Business, Telstra.
Naomi Rossdeutscher, Writer, Designer, House of Paradox.
Adam Savill, Partner, Tata Consulting Services.
Malcolm de Silva, Director Mining and Engineering, Microsoft.
Erica Smyth AC, NED MinEx CRC
Mark Stickells, Director, Pawsey Supercomputing Research Centre.
Damien Tampling, Global Chief Strategy Officer, Xero.
Paula Taylor, Ambassador, Global Blockchain Business Council.
Dr Natasha Teakle, Managing Director /Co-founder, AgriStart.
Peter Thompson, Senior Manager, AgTech, Graincorp.
Lina Velosa, Innovation Director, Fugro.
Rohan Workman, CEO and Founder, Skalata Ventures.

Bibliography

BOOKS

Anthony, Scott, and Gilbert, Clark and Johnson, Mark, 2017, Dual Transformation: How to Reposition Today's Business While Creating the Future.

Blainey, Geoffrey, 1966, The Tyranny of Distance: How Distance Shaped Australia's History.

Campbell, Andrew and Park, Robert, 2005, The Growth Gamble.

Christensen, Clayten and Raynor, Michael, 2013, The Innovator's Solution: Creating and Sustaining Successful Growth.

Christensen, Clayten, 1997, The Innovator's Dilemma: When New Technologies Cause Great Firms to Fail.

Collins, Jim, 2000, Good to Great: Why Some Companies Make the Leap and Others Don't.

Collins, Jim and Porras, Jerry, 2004, Built to Last: Successful Habits of Visionary Companies.

Diamandis, Peter and Kotler, Philip, 2016, Abundance: The Future Is Better Than You Think.

Gates, Bill, 2021, How to Avoid a Climate Disaster: The Solutions We Have and the Breakthroughs We Need.

Kim, W Chan and Mauborgne, Renée, 2015, Blue Ocean Strategy: How to create uncontested market space and make the competition irrelevant.

Kurtzweil, Ray, 2006, The Singularity is Near.

Moore Geoffrey, 2014, Crossing the Chasm.

Moore, Geoffrey, 2004, Inside the Tornado.

Ridley, Matt, 2011, The Rational Optimist: How Prosperity Evolves.

Ruffa, Simon, 2008, How the Best Companies Apply Lean Manufacturing Principles to Shatter Uncertainty, Drive Innovation, and Maximize Profits.

Silverstein, David and Phillip. Samuel and De Carlo, Neil, 2012, The Innovator's Toolkit: 50+ Techniques for Predictable and Sustainable Organic Growth.

Stephens-Davidowitz, Seth, 2018, Everybody Lies: What the Internet Can Tell Us About Who.

ARTICLES

National J Mass, The Relative Value of Growth, 2005.
https://hbr.org/2005/04/the-relative-value-of-growth

Uri Naren, What High Growth Companies Share in Common.
https://innovationmanagement.se/2013/03/22/what-high-growth-companies-share-in-common/

Anna Bedford, Le Mar, Nelson Mar, Christina Vojvoda, Future profitability and stock returns of innovative firms in Australia.
https://www.uts.edu.au/news/business-law/innovation-predicts-higher-profits-and-stock-returns

How VC's Look at Startups and Founders.
https://corporatefinanceinstitute.com/resources/valuation/how-vcs-look-at-startups-and-founders/

Austrade, Why Australia? Benchmark Report.
https://www.austrade.gov.au/benchmark-report/innovation-skills

McKinsey, 2021, Why 2021 will define the next decade for Australian companies.
https://www.mckinsey.com/capabilities/strategy-and-corporate-finance/our-insights/why-2021-will-define-the-next-decade-for-australian-companies

Steve Black, 2019, Why Companies and Government Do 'Innovation Theater' Instead of Actual Innovation.
https://steveblank.com/2019/10/15/between-a-rock-and-a-hard-place-organizational-and-innovation-theater/

Sarah Goff-Dupont, 2021, This is what a successful home-grown innovation program looks like.
https://www.atlassian.com/blog/technology/point-a-atlassian-innovation-program

Chargeoninnovation, BHP, Rio Tinto and Vale have come together to solve one of the biggest challenges in mining today to decarbonise mining operations. https://chargeoninnovation.com/

Josh Lerner, 2013, Corporate Venturing.
https://hbr.org/2013/10/corporate-venturing

Trevor Vas, 2015, SEEK talks about innovation and the changing employment marketplace.
https://atcevent.com/hr-tech/seek-talks-about-innovation-and-the-changing-employment-marketplace/

Patrick Forth and Stefan Gross-Selbeck, 2021, A Proven Model for Corporate Venturing.
https://www.bcg.com/publications/2022/corporate-venturing-models

Melissa Watson, 2021, How better managers can boost Australia's dynamism.
https://www.ceda.com.au/NewsAndResources/Opinion/Economy/How-better-managers-can-boost-Australias-business

Jeff Dyer, Nathan Furr, Curtis Lefrandt and Taeya Howell, 2023, Why Innovation Depends on Intellectual Honesty.
https://sloanreview.mit.edu/article/why-innovation-depends-on-intellectual-honesty/

Business Model Design and Innovation.
https://web.archive.org/web/20061213141941/http://business-model-design.blogspot.com/2005/11/what-is-business-model.html

McKinsey, 2016, Six secrets to true originality.
https://www.mckinsey.com/capabilities/people-and-organizational-performance/our-insights/six-secrets-to-true-originality

Alexandra Hall, Jason Inacio, Stephen O'Carroll and Guilherme Riederer, 2021, Australia and New Zealand: Building 'agile' capability.
https://www.mckinsey.com/capabilities/people-and-organizational-performance/our-insights/australia-and-new-zealand-building-agile-capability

Dashan Wang and James Evans, 2019, Research: When Small Teams Are Better Than Big Ones.
https://hbr.org/2019/02/research-when-small-teams-are-better-than-big-ones

CapGemini Consulting, The Foundations of Corporate Innovation in the Digital Age.
https://ide.mit.edu/wp-content/uploads/2018/05/The-foundations-of-corporate-innovation-in-the-digital-age.pdf?x96981

Gary Pisano, 2019, The Hard Truth About Innovative Cultures.
https://hbr.org/2019/01/the-hard-truth-about-innovative-cultures

Mike Bechtel, Khalid Kark, Nishita Henry, 2021, Innovation Study 2021: Beyond the buzzword.
https://www2.deloitte.com/us/en/insights/topics/innovation/corporate-innovation-program-report-and-key-takeaways.html

INDEX

3M, 52

Agile, 153-154

Amazon and/or AWS, 17, 21, 70-76, 137

Andreessen, Marc, 29-30

Apple, 138

Atlassian, 99, 110-111, 123, 137, 140

BHP, 40, 111, 124

Blue Ocean, 54-55

Business Model Canvas, 149-150

Canva, 135-136

CBA or Commbank, 40-41, 124

Christensen, Clayton, 35, 53-54, 136

Cochlear, 21, 33

Coles, 124

Collins, Jim, 131, 188

Crowd Innovation, 150-153

CSIRO, 41, 167-171

CSL, 112, 176, 187-188

Diamandis, Peter, 29, 58-59

Fugro, 87-88

Gates, Bill, 37-38

Google and/or Alphabet, 27-28, 59, 62

Graincorp, 60, 125, 160, 184

IAG, 126, 160

Imdex, 172, 176

Intel, 118-120

Kurtzweil, Ray, 25, 68

Lean Management, 153-154

Microsoft, 28

Mirvac, 162

Moore's Law, 23, 26

NAB, 125, 190-191

Pet Circle, 50

Proctor and Gamble, 159

Rio Tinto, 51, 151

SEEK, 88-89, 99, 126, 184

Skalata Ventures, 114, 129

Spaghetti marshmallow challenge, 194

Stan, 49

Telstra, 51-52, 113, 126

Who Gives a Crap, 20

Woodside Energy, 33, 86-87, 177, 186

Woolworths, 32, 39

Y Combinator, 104

Xero, 31, 99

1. The Franklin Institute: Edison''s Lightbulb. https://www.fi.edu/history-resources/edisons-lightbulb

2. National Museum of American History: Bread-slicing Machine. Accessed at: https://americanhistory.si.edu/collections/search/object/nmah_1317263

3. Bansi Najgi and Geoff Tuff, 2013, Managing your innovation portfolio. Accessed at: https://hbr.org/2012/05/managing-your-innovation-portfolio

4. Klaus Schwab, The Fourth Industrial Revolution. Accessed at: https://www.weforum.org/about/the-fourth-industrial-revolution-by-klaus-schwab

5. Fred Vogelstein, 2013, The Day Google Had to "Start Over" on Android. Accessed at: https://www.theatlantic.com/technology/archive/2013/12/the-day-google-had-to-start-over-on-android/282479/

6. Craig McLuckie, 2013, From Google to the world: The Kubernetes origin story. Accessed at: https://cloud.google.com/blog/products/containers-kubernetes/from-google-to-the-world-the-kubernetes-origin-story

7. Marc Andreessen, 2005, What software is eating the world. https://pdf4pro.com/view/why-software-is-eating-the-world-1bb986.html

8. Jeremy Preston, Ashley VanZeeland, Daniel Peiffer, 2005, Innovation at Illumina: The road to the $600 human genome. https://www.nature.com/articles/d42473-021-00030-9

9. Anna Curzon, 2018, How does Xero prioritise product improvements and feature requests? https://www.xero.com/blog/2019/12/how-xero-prioritises-product-improvements-and-requests/

10. IBM, Using IBM Watson technology to extract decades of experience from an ocean of data. https://www.ibm.com/case-studies/woodside-energy-watson-cognitive

11. GitHub, 2023, Your AI pair programme. https://github.com/features/copilot

12. Author interviews

13. Alex Edmans, 2022, The end of ESG. https://papers.ssrn.com/sol3/papers.cfm?abstract_id=4221990

14. OECD, Gross domestic spending on R&D. https://data.oecd.org/rd/gross-domestic-spending-on-r-d.htm

15. TopTal Talent Network, Three Core Principles of Venture Capital Portfolio Strategy. https://www.toptal.com/finance/venture-capital-consultants/venture-capital-portfolio-strategy

16. David Thodey's innovation action items for directors. https://www.aicd.com.au/good-governance/organisational-strategy/business-innovation/david-thodeys-innovation-action-items-for-directors.html

17. Ainsley Harris, 2023, How OpenAI's Mira Murati became one of techs most innovative leaders. https://www.fastcompany.com/90850342/openai-mira-murati-chatgpt-dall-e-gpt-4

18. Colin Brya and Bill Carr, 2021, Why (and How) Amazon Created the Kindle and Changed the Book Industry Forever. Accessed at: https://www.entrepreneur.com/growing-a-business/why-and-how-amazon-created-the-kindle-and-changed-the/363311

19. Boston Consulting Group, 2023, Reaching New Heights in Uncertain Times. https://www.bcg.com/publications/2023/advantages-through-innovation-in-uncertain-times

20. Justin Manly and Michael Ward; 2023; What Innovation Leaders Do Differently. https://www.bcg.com/publications/2023/what-innovation-leaders-do-differently

21. https://govhack.org/

22. Erik Larson, New Research: Diversity + Inclusion = Better Decision Making At Work. https://www.forbes.com/sites/eriklarson/2017/09/21/new-research-diversity-inclusion-better-decision-making-at-work/?sh=2f6e81b04cbf

23. 2022 Disney Accelerator Participants Announced. https://thewaltdisneycompany.com/2022-disney-accelerator-participants-announced/

24. Welcome to Area 120, Google's in-house incubator. https://area120.google.com/

25. Kenan Flagler, 2019, Do accelerators really work? https://www.kenan-flagler.unc.edu/news/do-accelerators-really-work/

26. Rachel Gutnick, 2022, Corporations Launched 140 Venture Capital Funds in 2021. https://medium.com/touchdownvc/corporations-launched-140-venture-capital-funds-in-2021-93372b1b061a#:~:text=Between%202011%20and%202021%2C%20annual,in%20venture%20capital%20also%20increased

27. Chirag Patel and Iliya Rybchin, 2022, Corporate venture capital (CVC): A critical driver for enterprise growth in turbulent times. https://www.ey.com/en_us/growth/why-corporate-venture-capital-programs-are-more-important-than-ever

28. Patrick Haslanger, Erik E. Lehmann and Nikolaus Seitz, The performance effects of corporate venture capital: a meta-analysis. https://link.springer.com/article/10.1007/s10961-022-09954-w

29. Greg Watson, 2023, Changing investor attitudes are creating an opportunity for CVC. https://globalventuring.com/corporate/changing-investor-cvc/

30. David Horowitz, 2019, Five Reasons Corporate Venture Capital Programs Fail. https://medium.com/touchdownvc/five-reasons-corporate-venture-capital-programs-fail-cace36f1191e

31. James Manning, 2023, Mediaweek, The future of Foxtel. https://www.mediaweek.com.au/the-future-of-foxtel-chief-executive-patrick-delany-on-maintaining-momentum/

32. BCA and CSIRO, 2021, Unlocking the innovation potential of Australian companies. https://www.bca.com.au/unlocking_the_innovation_potential_of_australian_companies

33. Ramón Baeza, David Allred, Michael Brigl, Sandra Deutschländer, Charles Gildehaus, Deborah Lovich, Matthias Schmidt, Chris Stutzman, and Lauren Taylor, 2021, Most Innovative Companies 2021. https://www.bcg.com/publications/2021/understanding-ceo-innovation

34. Global Innovation Index, 2021.
    https://www.wipo.int/edocs/pubdocs/en/wipo_pub_gii_2021/au.pdf

35. CSIRO, 2021, Unlocking the innovation potential of Australian companies.
    https://www.csiro.au/en/work-with-us/services/consultancy-strategic-advice-services/CSIRO-futures/Innovation-Business-Growth/Unlocking-innovation-potential

36. AlphaBeta, 2020. Australian Business Investment.
    https://www.industry.gov.au/sites/default/files/2020-02/australian-business-investment-in-innovation-levels-trends-and-drivers.pdf

37. Characteristics of Australian Business, 2020,
    https://www.abs.gov.au/statistics/industry/technology-and-innovation/characteristics-australian-business/latest-release

38. Erik Larson, New Research: Diversity + Inclusion = Better Decision Making At Work.
    https://www.forbes.com/sites/eriklarson/2017/09/21/new-research-diversity-inclusion-better-decision-making-at-work/?sh=2f6e81b04cbf

39. CSIRO and University of Queensland, 2020, Thriving Through Innovation: Lessons from the Top. https://www.csiro.au/en/work-with-us/services/consultancy-strategic-advice-services/csiro-futures/innovation-business-growth/thriving-through-innovation

40. Jordan Bar Am, Felicitas Jorge, Laura Furstenthal and Erik Roth, 2020, Innovation in a crisis. https://www.mckinsey.com/capabilities/strategy-and-corporate-finance/our-insights/innovation-in-a-crisis-why-it-is-more-critical-than-ever

41. AICD and the University of Sydney, 2022, Innovation in the boardroom: Rising to the challenge? https://www.aicd.com.au/content/dam/aicd/pdf/news-media/research/2022/innovation-in-the-boardroom-2022-web.pdf

42. Atlassian, 2021, How to Invent the Future. https://atlassianblog.wpengine.com/wp-content/uploads/2021/04/atlassian-guide-culture-of-innovation.pdf

www.ingramcontent.com/pod-product-compliance
Lightning Source LLC
Chambersburg PA
CBHW062046290426
44109CB00027B/2744